Her Own Woman

PROFILES OF TEN CANADIAN WOMEN

by MYRNA KOSTASH,
MELINDA McCRACKEN,
VALERIE MINER,
ERNA PARIS,
HEATHER ROBERTSON

Macmillan of Canada   Toronto

ISBN 0-7705-1275-5

Printed in Canada for
The Macmillan Company of Canada
70 Bond Street, Toronto M5B 1X3

Contents

For our mothers
and our children—
Michelle, Roland, Molly and Aaron

ERRATA

1. In the chapter entitled KATHLEEN: AMAZON DAUGHTER several paragraphs have been transposed through a printer's error.

   On page 50 the second paragraph ("Well, the deadpan of that delivery" etc.) has been transposed. Everything from that point until the end of the second paragraph on page 52 ("kind of growing up.") should appear on page 54 between the first paragraph ("flat-chested.") and the next one beginning "The break had been made".

2. In the chapter entitled PORTRAIT OF BARBARA, on page 171 the second paragraph ("We never talked about that" etc.) has been transposed. It should appear as the third paragraph on page 170, between the end of the second paragraph ("at a different time.") and the start of the following one ("Then I remember the day" etc.).

Introduction

This book was started on a warm, spring-like evening in March, 1973, at a small gathering in a Toronto apartment. The four of us, Myrna Kostash, Melinda McCracken, Valerie Miner, and Erna Paris, had a lot in common. We were all reasonably young, we were all professional magazine writers, and we had all come through (or were coming through) the upheaval of the women's movement in the late 60s and early 70s.

We passed around a bottle of Szekszardi wine and talked small talk until the conversation turned to the kind of writing that was coming out of the women's movement. And we discovered that we had all become bored with the theme of woman as victim that so much of this writing seemed to project. That women had been and still were oppressed in different ways was a fact none of us disputed, but we felt that that condition had already been exhaustively documented in terms of women's personal lives. We thought, indeed, we *knew* that there were women around who lived successful personal lives, in spite of the difficulties they encountered. We ourselves had overcome personal and social obstacles in our own lives, and we were making our way more or less smoothly in the free-for-all of the journalistic marketplace.

Someone suggested that an encounter between us and other energetic, expressive women would make an interesting book, as much for the style of highly personal, involved, and opinionated journalism we would write it in as for the stories of courage and imagination the book would relate. From these profiles a picture of Canadian women might or might not emerge, but the experience would be worthwhile on its own.

During the following weeks, the book idea began to take hold. We tested it out on Robert Fulford, the editor at *Saturday Night* and got a positive response. Bob had been important to several of us at the beginning of our writing careers. He had encouraged us, worked with us, and published us when we had few or no credits to our names. Heather Robertson agreed to join us, as did Susan Kent, an experienced book editor. Susan Feldman, the editor of the Toronto Star's *Star Week* agreed to act as a combination literary agent and general manager.

As the planning for the book became more precise, it was decided that each writer would contribute two articles. We talked and argued, but in the end we felt that our subjects should represent a mix of famous and anonymous women, because the ability to take charge of one's life is clearly not limited to the celebrated. Nor is it limited to one age group, or to the middle-class.

So we chose a distinctly varied group of women. Not all are flamboyant militants in the feminist avant-garde. Far from it. Some would firmly reject such a description of themselves, and settle for something as reasonable and peaceable as equal rights. Some would put the question in purely personal terms—what have *I* been, seen, done, and what do *I* want. Some have made their peace by creating a small region of security and love where they do their work, and others will not rest until a whole cultural fabric is replaced by a new social order. Some are married, some have been, and some never will be. Some have been successful in socially-approved ways, others emphatically have not. But where they are all alike is that, in one way or another, they have refused to play victim in the war of attrition with sexism. With small and grand gestures they have become as completely themselves as possible, and to that extent they are independent and self-determining persons; each person you will meet in this book is her own woman.

For us, for the writers, one of the most interesting aspects of this book was the way it was written. We decided to attempt a co-operative venture—and it worked, given a few tensions here and there. Each of the articles was circulated among all the members of the group, and then at regular meetings that began in October, 1973 and ended in the spring of 1974, we sat in each other's living rooms and discussed, edited, applauded, criticized, and generally pulled apart each other's work. Given the egos involved when writers expose their wares, it was a perilous experiment—and, on the whole, it worked splendidly.

We've taken the space to talk about this book's background because it *was* experimental, and because we hope that our encounters with ten strong and courageous women will touch other people, just as they touched us.

The Honourable Judy

BY HEATHER ROBERTSON

Judy LaMarsh leans forward in her armchair, blinking slightly in the glare of the TV studio lights. "You are known as a manure distributor," she says, fixing her male guest with an eye blurred and magnified by glasses thick as the bottoms of pop bottles. "What makes you tick?" The man squirms, blushes coyly and makes goldfish motions with his mouth. Judy waits, silent. She fills the armchair, still fat but slimmer now than the obese woman who quit the Pearson government in 1968; her face is pale, moon-like, her glasses owlish hornrims, her hair, the bane of her existence, cropped short. When the man finally answers she beams on him with her radiant smile, the ear-to-ear smile which transforms her suddenly into a beautiful woman. "I always smile for pictures," she says, "because my face in repose looks like I'm going to tear the head off somebody."

At 50 she is still the familiar Judy of the newspaper photographs and cartoons, but older, more mature, relaxed. She is still tough, aggressive, abrasive, but the anger and defensiveness have diminished; she radiates confidence, good will, and control, a far different woman from the tense, hostile mountain of green brocade in black fishnet stockings I met during her last election campaign in 1965. She is stripped down, bereft of the blonde wigs and three-inch dangling earrings, the feathered hats and strings of clunky beads that made her a grotesque parakeet, devoid now of the silver lamé stockings and red vinyl boots in which she used to show off her shapely legs. Instead there's a cartoon on the door of her office at Osgoode Hall Law School in Toronto showing a man with his trousers rolled up over his knobby knees and a female executive saying "Hire him, he has marvellous legs." Five years as the only woman in the Liberal cabinet ("Pearson said that one of me enlivened a cabinet, while two would have convulsed it") has made Judy LaMarsh into one of Canada's most ardent advocates for women's rights.

"Being in the government matured me, *fast!*" she says. "I was pretty idealistic about politics up until then. Most ministers who leave government go on to half a dozen boards and their friends rally around. That certainly didn't happen to *me*. I've never even been offered an appointment by the government. I looked for a job in Toronto and was rebuffed because I was a woman. Oh, I've had lots of frustration but I always thought it was limited to myself. It came as one of the biggest surprises to find there were others who had the same frustrations. I always used to think, well, there's nothing I can do about it. That's the way things are. I found out there are lots of things that can be changed. I've been very lucky in having opportunities to put to work some of the things I've learned. I've been able to grow."

Instead of fading into genteel retirement when she left the government after five years as Minister of National Health and Welfare and Secretary of State, Judy wrote her autobiography, *Memoirs of a Bird in a Gilded Cage*, an explosive account of her years as a Liberal MP which established her as a merciless political critic and instant literary celebrity. She had her own TV show in Ottawa and took a job as host of a radio hotline program in Vancouver, the most brutally competitive market in Canada, where she quickly topped the king, Jack Webster, in the ratings. "I wasn't as much of a success as people seem to think," she says. "I was a success in so far as I went to the hottest market and I didn't fall on my nose—which I guess people expected I would. I know that every time I take on something different, the odds shorten on the time I'm gonna fall on my nose. And I keep thinking 'I wonder if this is it?'"

In 1974 she returned east to teach law at Osgoode Hall, the quiet, respectable school from which she had graduated as president of her class in 1950. "I think it would be nice just to teach, but I would probably go nuts," she says. "Besides, I can't afford to teach unless I do a lot of other things." Her schedule is staggering: she is a director of Unity Bank and a member of a dozen committees; the phone-in television show takes two hours every Sunday night, she writes a weekly column for the *Toronto Star* and appears frequently as a political commentator on CBC radio. Judy turns up at meetings for reform in family and divorce law, attends Canadian Legion think-ins and hires herself out as guest speaker for everything from the Canadian Bar Association to the manufacturers of frozen foods. "The speeches and kinds of things I'm being asked to do are more *establishment* now," she says with satisfaction. "I'm much more respectable."

"Judy is *everywhere*," says a magazine editor. "What's she up to?"

Her phone rings. She haggles about money. "Call me back when you find out how much you can pay," she says, banging down the receiver. Judy is very hardnosed about money. It shocks some people. "Some people think an ex-cabinet minister should just sit on her honourable behind and starve," she says. She earns a lot and spends a lot, but for things she believes in her time is free. A defeated candidate calls, unemployed. Judy suggests jobs and they chortle over some hot political gossip. The CBC calls. Then an old friend. Can he come for dinner? Judy leafs through her calendar, frowning. Every moment of every day is booked solid. "Good food and lotsa booze," she promises, picking a date a month away. She rubs the fatigue from her eyes, lights a cigarette and takes a long drag.

"What makes you tick?" I ask. She grins. "Momentum, I guess."

The telephone is almost an extension of her arm. Judy is engaged in a continuous conversation. She talks in a slangy vernacular, slurring words together, dropping her g's, speaking a tough-kid street language liberally laced with mild profanity which tends to conceal her intelligence and identify her with the common man. The phone is at once her lifeline and her barricade; it keeps her in touch with personal and political friends, the most important people in her life, yet the incessant chatter, the frantic ritual of busyness, the tangle of appointments, also defends her from intrusion, from the tediousness of fools, and the solitude of her own thoughts.

Trying to meet Judy I feel I am hacking my way through the Enchanted Forest towards the Sleeping Beauty. Even at the end, after weeks of dogged perseverance, the final encounter remains dubious, uncertain. "You want to see me?" she says casually, brushing by as I sit patiently by her office door. I am cast in the role of humble supplicant, courtier, lover; my voice is small, almost apologetic, my manner diffident. I seek to please. I find myself down on my knees plugging in the coffee pot. There is no doubt about who is the stronger woman. I don't mind; she's earned it. There is an intimate, almost sensual tension in the air; Judy has a ruthless, egocentric, theatrical quality, a quality represented by her real name—Julia Verlyn LaMarsh ("My name," she said once, "sounds like something that should be up in lights over a strip tease theatre.") I am Alice before the Queen of Hearts. Perhaps it is her voice, a husky contralto that drops off at the end of phrases, but I think of Mae West's famous invitation; there is something of the courtesan about Judy. I can understand now why men are fascinated by her power and terrified of her sting, and how this ambivalent relationship first made her outstandingly successful in politics, and then almost destroyed her.

Judy LaMarsh is one of the most influential women in Canada; during her years in cabinet she wielded power on a scale unsurpassed by any other Canadian woman. As Minister of Health and Welfare she implemented the Canada Pension Plan and designed medicare; as Secretary of State she brought in a new Broadcasting Act, initiated reform within the CBC with an off-the-cuff remark about "rotten management", set up the Royal Commission on the Status of Women and presided over Canada's brilliantly successful Centennial. Within five years she was responsible for almost all the most memorable and innovative legislation of the Pearson government. When Pearson retired in 1968, she quit.

"There was nowhere I could go. It was just not in the cards that Mike or anyone like him was going to make me Minister of Justice or that I was ever going to be able to run for Prime Minister. I had had very intensive experience and after that it was just going to be routine. When people talk to me about going back into politics—to do *what*?"

Judy first ran for election to the House of Commons in a 1960 by-election. She was 35 and one of the "nice people" of Niagara Falls, as she puts it. She had practiced law with her father, W.C. LaMarsh, a dyed-in-the-wool Liberal, for 10 years ("We fought like cats and dogs all the time") and belonged to just about every civic and charitable organization in Niagara Falls, as well as holding office in the young Liberals, the Liberal women, and the Liberal Party of Canada. She had earned her crack at the nomination.

She organized her constituency thoroughly, starting with the women, and campaigned aggressively in the factories. "I was," she says, "no namby-pamby female afraid to speak up for her constituents." She won by 5000 votes; her opponent just saved his deposit, the only one who ever has. Although she was elected to the House of Commons at the nadir of Liberal strength, only one senior party member, George McIlraith, phoned to offer congratulations. She discovered that she was, as she was to learn bitterly during her eight years in Ottawa, alone.

"No one on the Liberal side gave less of a damn whether I was there or not. So many of Mr. Pearson's backbenchers were really office holders and that's all. They played bridge all the time. The only strength he had was on the front row. So I sat there for a month and then I started to talk. They were a little surprised. In this men's club they thought women were there on sufferance, that it was a freak election that I got there, and I ought to be modestly pleased with that and not try to contribute."

Judy had enthusiasm, a passionate devotion to the Liberal party, and the gift of all great politicians, an unerring instinct for a hot political issue: an army veteran and hawk on military matters, she was aware of the Diefenbaker government's weakness on defense long before the Liberal hierarchy. She urged Pearson to take a stand in favour of accepting nuclear arms for Canada's NATO forces, the issue which would catapult the Liberals back into power in the 1963 election. Her reward during the election campaign was appointment to the Truth Squad. "One of the things that has been my undoing in politics," she wrote in her memoirs, "is my readiness to do whatever job has to be done. The dirty jobs of politics often fell to me." The Truth Squad was a dirty job; along with two other Liberal watchdogs, she was assigned to attend Diefenbaker rallies to point out inaccuracies in his speeches. Diefenbaker crucified her. "I never made any record of his witticisms at my expense," she wrote, "but I still bear their scars." The Truth Squad lasted an uproarious five nights and Judy became a national joke. Stripped of her dignity, she was fair game for a hostile male press which stalked her mercilessly for the next five years.

Do you think, I ask her, that women are often set up as punching bags to take abuse, or expected to act as lightning rods for criticism, because they are considered expendable? "I wouldn't be surprised," she says wryly. "I remember Jimmy Sinclair telling me, 'they're making you the sledge hammer of the party. Don't let them do it. They'll turn you into a battle axe.' "

When the Liberals formed the government after the election Judy was appointed to the health and welfare ministry. "I had always assumed that if I made it to Parliament I would not remain a backbencher," she says. "I would have been surprised, hurt, and damned mad if I had not been included." She was strong, intelligent, with 18 years of service to the Liberal Party, and she was the only woman. "I have never looked for prejudice," she stated confidently in 1963, "and I have never run into it." She wore feathered hats, stiletto-heel shoes, strings of pearls, and sensible schoolteacher dresses, and looked for all the world like a successful clubwoman of 1955.

"The No. 1 Spinster in Canada", *Weekend* magazine hailed her in 1964. The article, by Angela Burke, informed us that Miss LaMarsh, "looking suitably careerish wearing an uncluttered blond knit", was 5'7", owned a white Thunderbird with red upholstery, had a poodle called Mimi, smoked three packs of cigarettes a day, did needlepoint, cooked an excellent beef stroganoff, and had gained 30 pounds since she had been in the cabinet. A sheepish Judy was photographed in front of her bedroom mirror with her collection of perfume bottles. "She puts on a show of single blessedness," meowed Miss Burke. For Judy it was a choice between this simpering women's-page stuff and the vicious barbs of columnists like Doug Fisher, a former classmate from the University of Toronto, who described her as "an odd bod", a drill sergeant in jack boots, "a dreadnought-sized Charlotte Whitton". Her old friend, Liberal bagman Keith Davey, said: "She gets crushes, not in the boy-girl sense, but someone comes into her orbit and she's overwhelmed—for the time being." No one knew how to deal with Judy outside the conventional stereotypes—she was a twittering old maid or she was butch. (When Pauline Jewett became a Liberal MP in 1965, the joke went around Ottawa that she was a "female Judy LaMarsh".) When Judy was appointed Secretary of State in 1965, Charles Lynch wrote that she had many fine qualities but "cultured she ain't".

"I am not a boor," replied Judy, hurt and shocked. "I go to art shows. I enjoy theatre and opera and ballet. I listen to music." She was seldom praised; adjectives applied to her were pejorative—"colourful", "bombastic"—even when they meant to flatter. "I don't believe I am a shrew," said Judy, puzzled, "but I am always cast in the attacking role." She deliberately avoided criticizing Conservative MP Ellen Fairclough ("I thought men would be amused to see a couple of women pulling hair") and refused to campaign against Conservative women candidates. She was socially ostracized by her cabinet colleagues and other MP's ("I doubt that I had lunch with one or another of my colleagues in an informal way more than a handful of times. They simply didn't think of calling me, and I hesitated to call them"), cut off from contact with people, isolated by her position from normal relationships with men.

"It was sexual hostility, a feeling that I was a bull in a china shop, not only that but it was a male china shop and I should just not draw attention to my presence. The wives were hostile too. I was a lot better-looking in those days and I think I let myself get fat as much as anything to do something about that. I've noticed since I've looked like this that there's practically no hostility from women. I guess they don't think I'm any kind of challenge.

"Women made me uncomfortable. I really didn't know women until I got out of government. I had school friends but I had never formed any female friendships in my adult years. I had a great friend in college and she lived in Ottawa. We had lunch together one day and never saw each other after that. Maybe they felt diminished and threatened by me. I haven't any idea. I was scared of them, because my life had been so different. I had lived in a male world since I was 18, in the army, in college. As a lawyer I rarely ran into women except as legal secretaries. I worked a lot at night and my friends had young children, so we didn't see much of each other."

Judy was the second of three children. A family portrait at the age of four shows a blasé, knowing little girl with a round face and blonde ringlets. Her youth in Chatham, Ontario, and Niagara Falls was in every way respectable. She was not a brilliant student and did better at athletics than she did at exams. "My mother told me I used to collect brides when I was a kid, millions of pictures of brides. I don't even *like* weddings." She read movie magazines, kept a diary in French, which she spoke as a secret language with her girlfriends ("In Niagara Falls it *was* a secret language") and worried about boys.

"I didn't date very much at high school. I was, I suppose, late in coming to any awareness of boys in that way. I was always everybody's friend, taught them all how to dance, and popular, popular in things like elected office and stuff. I would have two or three male friends and I always had a date for a dance or something, but they weren't the football heroes or anything else. I'm sure I was about the third or fourth person they'd asked. And that distressed me when I was in high school. My mother said, 'You're the kind of person who'll be more popular when you're older.' I wasn't experimental about sex. God, I think I was a virgin until I was about 27! And that's after I was in the army from 18 to 21!

"I always wanted to be a lawyer. I don't think my father ever accepted that I was going to be a lawyer until I'd left college and went to Osgoode. I had never discussed it with him. I had always planned to go to university. I had *assumed* it. When I graduated from high school my dad said, 'No. I can't do that, I don't have the money and your brother is coming along.' He came first. My brother went to university. He only went for a year. He decided it was only to play football and quit. It was the biggest shock of my life, to be told I couldn't go to university."

She was turned down by the airforce when she couldn't see

the eye chart without her glasses and spent a year at teachers' college; in 1942 she enlisted in the army at 18. She served in Halifax, Vancouver, and Washington, D.C. "It was a very happy experience. I still love uniforms and people in uniform. I couldn't live in the army now, it doesn't fit me now, but the army was good to me. I was a girl from a parochial family living with one class of people all my life—I sure got to learn all sorts of things." Judy studied drafting, which had been forbidden her in high school because she was female, and was one of a handful of women selected to learn Japanese. As it was for many women, the war was a tremendously liberating experience. "It was the biggest thing happening in the world," she says, "and I didn't want to be out of it!"

When she got out of the service in 1945, she wanted to be a civil engineer. She was told no. Her counsellor said she couldn't get a job as an engineer. "I was told I could always get a job as a lawyer because my dad was a lawyer."

The army paid her way to university and it was at the University of Toronto that she became a Liberal. "I was sitting and talking to a couple of women in the coffee shop one night and they introduced me to a great big good-looking guy and he said, 'Why don't you join the Liberal Club?' I didn't know anybody at college so I said okay, I'll go and maybe I'll meet some people, so I did. Some of those people have been lifelong friends."

"My grandfather had been a passionate Grit and my dad turned the riding Liberal for the first time. I remember my grandfather sitting with tears running down his cheeks when Mitch Hepburn was elected. It impressed me that something about politics was very important."

Her father died in 1957, her mother in 1960. Politics became her life.

"I was never any intellectual giant. When I was going to run I went to a thinkers' conference to find out if I really was a Liberal. I enjoyed it and I got at what the party is. Same thing as being a Presbyterian. I've always been a Presbyterian. When I was at teachers' college we had to take lectures in religious instruction and I was quite astonished to find out what a Presbyterian *was!*"

On the train to Ottawa to take her seat in the House, Judy was cautioned by an elderly lawyer from St. Catharines. "You are a very young woman in a very important position," he told her. "You must watch yourself because you're the image of all women."

To be a woman, she discovered, was not necessarily to be a lady. Responsible for steering the complex and controversial Canada Pension Plan through the House, Judy found herself embroiled in bitter public warfare with the insurance industry and with provincial premiers anxious to indulge in a little public grandstanding and muscle-flexing. With a quick, precise, and logical mind and absolutely no tolerance for bombast or bullshit, Judy found all the wheeling and dealing tedious and frustrating; she found, too, that a well-timed fit of rage could speed the ponderous progress of the ship of state.

She wrote about the process in her book. "Perhaps because they were sorry for me (a hateful thing to me, to be an object of pity, but sometimes useful) or perhaps because they were afraid of me (I was mad and moody and didn't hide what I thought of the whole damned Quebec compromise, which left me looking like an ass) they went along with two things I'd been trying to get included. . . . But it took the shine off politics for me, and in the minds of many stamped me as a quarrelsome, stubborn, heavy-handed fighter. That's an unpleasant public image for anyone, especially a woman, and I resented it. I suppose, as a politician, I should be content, for the Canada Pension Plan certainly put my name in Canada's history books, and in italics." For Judy that distinction between "woman" and "politician" was to disappear.

In 1965, when she had just completed the spade work for the medicare legislation, Judy was peremptorily transferred to

Secretary of State. She saw it as a demotion. "Everything was in a terrible mess. The Centennial was disgraceful. It was used as a stuffing place for all kinds of people they didn't know what to do with. Nobody would *do* anything!" Pearson was desperate for someone strong enough to pull the Centennial out of the ashcan, or he was using her as a pawn, a commando unit who would charge in and get things moving and who, if things did not go well, could be left holding the bag. "I don't think Pearson thought the Centennial was going to be a success. I don't think any of them thought Expo was going to be a success. They were all waiting for the financial bricks to fall. I think Pearson thought the Centennial was going to be a damn bore with all those trips from heads of state, all those dinners and things." She would have preferred to be Minister of Defence. "He would have flipped before he'd have done that!"

Exhausted by the multifarious details of the Centennial, depressed and outraged by the political destruction of her closest friends in cabinet, Walter Gordon and Guy Favreau, Judy had another can of worms dumped in her lap: The CBC abruptly cancelled the popular and controversial television show, "This Hour Has Seven Days". Judy didn't like the show, but the decision offended her respect for free speech and she sided firmly with the producers. "Yellow journalism is not illegal," she said. "One has to collect news in any way one's stomach can bear." A year later her casual reference to "rotten management" once more blew the lid off the corporation.

"I told Mike to stay out of it. I got into it on my own and if I can't get out of it, you know what you can do. Let me handle it. The first two or three days I took absolute shit in the House. And then the cards and letters and phone calls started coming in and they shifted right around. Then I was afraid it was going to be a 100 per cent attack on the CBC and destroy the corporation, and I'm a great believer in public broadcasting."

In a government rocked by scandal, Judy acquired a reputation for uncompromising honesty; in a parliament littered with the victims of political assassinations and suicides, she emerged as a winner with a genius for the popular public gesture. (When Judy quit smoking to publicize the danger of cigarettes she made headlines for six weeks as the press followed her around to see if she was sneaking a puff.) Because the normal avenues of power were blocked to her, she retained her sense of distance from the political machine, and this perspective gave her an enormous advantage. "This isn't my career, it's a period in my life," she told a reporter in 1964. "As a consequence I don't take myself as seriously as do most male politicians. I can afford to gamble. A man can't." In 1967 at the peak of her power and celebrity, Judy decided to leave politics.

"I got so tired of fighting." The ceaseless grind of work, the loneliness, the glare of publicity, the constant scrape of controversy wearied her and sapped her confidence. She had no one to draw strength from. "There's no one to talk to about things," she said, "and, when you come right down to facts, nobody really cares if you live or die."

"It hurt when I saw something stinky about myself. Walter Gordon told me to stop reading the papers, stop looking at the cartoons. There's nothing like waking up in the morning and getting kicked in the ass. Starts the day off great." She began to feel rootless, alienated. "I feel like a piece of tumbleweed," she told a reporter. "I'd like to have my face back." Photographs taken in 1967 show a tired, fat, frumpy woman who looks years older than 43. She had won, but at what price?

"It warped my personality. I was really bitchy and always tired and short-tempered. God, I remember things—I'd throw things around. I fired my executive assistant once. He got out the door and I went after him and said, 'Christ, I'm not going to cut off both arms and legs. Come back here!' And he was big enough to come back. I don't think I was an easy person to be with or to work for. I *know* I wasn't. I've heard people tell tales to me now that make my hair stand on end, tales which I'd mercifully forgotten. Surely I never did *that*; but it must be true."

Like many women in a male world Judy felt she had to prove she was tough, that she could take it like a man; she became, as the sign on the door of her Vancouver radio studio read, "a steel-jacketed marshmallow". Judy adopted super-feminine wigs and bizarre costumes as camouflage; they only increased the publicity and ridicule. By the time of her hysterical performance at the Liberal leadership convention in 1968 when she called Trudeau a "bastard" on national TV, the stereotype had become real. Judy was a caricature of herself.

Listening to her talk and remembering the pain of a similar period in my own experience, I am impressed by her exposure, her vulnerability. How many of us have been through that kind of fire, alone, unshielded by convention, testing ourselves, pushing ourselves to the limits of our endurance and then beyond, harrassed by critics, hounded by gossip and rumour, our private lives turned inside-out, watching our friends being destroyed by the system in which we're struggling to stay alive, faced constantly by a mirror which shows an exaggerated and distorted image—yet, exhilarated at the same time by power, by the ability to alter the destiny of a nation, challenging the limits of our intelligence, knowing the anxiety of responsibility and the joy of creativity? Most of us cower on the sidelines. Few of us who dare, survive unbroken or unmaimed. Yet it has made Judy stronger; it has not hardened her but opened her.

Judy has no small talk, no aimless posturing to grease the wheels of social contact; she is without front or hypocrisy, direct, straightforward. She has no secrets. She can be blunt to the point of rudeness, confiding to the point of embarrass-ment. She has no public self and private self; in every encounter she is personally committed. Every person she meets is a potential friend or enemy: the decision is made very quickly and is usually irrevocable. She is emotionally and psychically on the line; it's a dangerous way to live. I think, strangely, of Marilyn Monroe, another star who lived entirely in the public eye and was destroyed by it. Judy survived, and survived on her own terms.

"I've always stood up for myself," she says. "I don't think I've picked any fights in Parliament. I didn't back down from any, either. I probably blew up more than anyone in cabinet, but when it's over I hold no grudges and carry no chips." She shies away from self-analysis with a shrug and "I dunno" and dismisses theorizing as so much gumflapping. She is a woman of action, a warrior and statesman; her values are Roman— justice, courage, truth, and loyalty. It is an unusual and revolutionary credo for a woman in our society; Judy has lived it and has broken a path for other women through the hoary and absurd conventions of Canadian politics. Why should a woman *not* be proud, ambitious, aggressive, angry in the face of deceit, contemptuous of stupidity, intolerant of corruption and, if she's a politician, ruthless, manipulative, egocentric? Judy learned quickly that she was smarter, more efficient, and a better politician than most of her male colleagues. Why should she suffer fools and bores meekly, or smile and take a back seat, or do the dirty work? There is nothing of the slave in Judy. She no longer takes pride in her ability to do the joe jobs of politics, nor is she apologetic about being unmarried.

"I've never had it in my mind that I was going to raise children and be a housewife. Not because I have anything against it; I have to keep my own house and I like to cook and design interiors—but I don't want to pick up wet socks and towels and clean off babies' bottoms. It just doesn't interest me at all. Some people have a very loving nature, and to do those things are signs of love and it fulfills them to do it. I'd rather not do it if I can avoid it. I was engaged for about three days while I was a law student to a naval officer because I thought it would be such a gas that he would only be around one month of the year." Her priorities have always been clear. "It would be completely unfair to have a husband," she said in 1964, "and to have him tagging around after a cabinet minister."

Judy has gone underground politically, biding her time, confronting her prejudices ("I can't get over that I believe that people who rape-murder small children should hang. And it's just sheer native vindictiveness, that's all. As primitive a feeling as anyone can get, and I can't get past it") and thinking more deeply about political ideology.

As I get older I have more streaks of conservatism, but I'm more left than right. I am left of the Liberal Party in most things. Trudeau is more Tory than Stanfield. My party left me. I didn't leave it." She is more politicized than she was 10 years ago, more realistic, cynical even, but she is still a Liberal and absolutely devoted to the game of politics.

"I seriously toyed with the idea of coming back to run as Ontario Liberal leader. I think I have a lot of the qualities Mitch Hepburn had, maybe the ones that destroyed him as well as the ones that got him there. With the right financial support—you're talking $1 million to $2 million—I thought I could well bring the Liberals within striking distance. Part of the trouble with politics is, like with Stanfield, who *wants* to lead that bunch of bums?"

In 1974 she teetered on the verge of running once more in her old Niagara Falls seat. One main consideration held her back: "Pierre would not promise that I would be in the cabinet." Yet she still spends every free weekend in Niagara Falls, mending fences. What's she up to? Prime Minister?

"Pooh," she shrugs. "I don't think that's very likely. And I don't really know that I would like it. I think I have practically no qualities to be Prime Minister, qualities like not being stampeded, and being long-headed and calm as well as responsible. I have never had any difficulty making up my mind, but I have had difficulty being *right*, and I still do."

Judy wanted to run for the Liberal leadership in 1968 and felt she would have made a creditable showing. The candidacy of a woman was not taken seriously by the party. "I would have been looked upon as a spoiler and an interloper," she says. She stayed out. She is intensely aware of her enormous popular appeal, her ability to reach people intimately and to understand their concerns instinctively—everyone naturally calls her "Judy". She is a powerful presence. People respond to her viscerally: they fear and respect her, love her and hate her. "People see something reflected in me, " she says. "They see in me what they want to see." There is something primitive, archetypal in the relationship: she is sun and moon, Great White Mother, Virgin Queen, and bitch goddess all in one, dangerous and unpredictable, yet at the same time strong and wise. It is this ambivalent quality that makes the public want to possess her, to worship and destroy her, a quality that becomes more irresistible the more she proclaims her independence.

"I don't belong to the party, nor the people," she says. "I am my own woman now."

The Heart of The Family

BY MELINDA McCRACKEN

When I was home for Christmas in Winnipeg one year, my family was invited for dinner at the home of another family who are close friends. Afterwards, the kids and the parents, replete with the customary feast, lay sunk in chairs around the Christmas tree. In the midst of the banter, the two moms, mellow on the wine and liqueurs the parents have lately taken to, wrapped their arms around each other's shoulders like two old army buddies and belted out:

"M is the for the million things she gave me
O means only that she's growing old
T is for the tears she shed to save me
H is for her heart of purest gold
E is everything she's done to help me
R means right and right she'll always be
Put them all together, they spell MOTHER
A word that means the wo-orld to me."

The song, which was popular during the First World War, is one that could only pop into the consciousnesses of two moms feeling sentimental with their broods assembled around them at a Christmas party. If nobody's going to remember them, they'll remember themselves.

My mom and her army buddy are typical middle-class Canadian moms. On the Christmas night in question, both were dressed "to the nines" as they'd say, their mom in a long hostess skirt and red top, her grey hair in one variation of a

19

French roll, and my mom in a short red dress with a corsage of glass baubles pinned at the neck, her blonde hair in her own version of a French roll. Both had interpreted it as their duty on the occasion to personify the Christmas spirit for their families. That's the way it is with moms—at Christmastime, they dress like Mrs. Santa Claus; on St. Patrick's Day, they're in their green; they've always got a Valentine for you; and on birthdays, it's steak, frozen strawberries, and a Dominion Store cake with roses and your name on it in icing.

Both moms grew up in small prairie towns, went to Normal school, and taught school in the country. There they met men who were school teachers, married them, and moved into the city. Both are the moms of grown-up children, and both now lead comfortable lives, well-rounded in the traditional manner. They do volunteer work in the traditional charity style—my mom works with the guild of the Princess Elizabeth Hospital for the chronically ill, and with groups in the church. They go to ballet, theatre, and symphony performances, and take extension courses at the University of Manitoba for their cultural input. They curl and go south in the winter, golf and go to "the lake" in the summer, and are addicted to bridge all year round.

They are the moms who grew up in Victorian Manitoba, whose style retains vestiges of "Old Country" customs: oatmeal for breakfast; fruit cake at bridge parties; afternoon teas; cycles of well-done roast beef, potatoes, vegetables, and brown gravy; and the baking of scones, baking powder biscuits, date loaves, and dainties. At the cottage, they love to put on jackets and pants and scarves and go off down the road, banging on a saucepan to keep away the bears. They disappear into the bushes, oblivious of the thistles and the mosquitoes whining around their heads, and the moving leaves and the cheerful humming from within indicate that there's a berry-picking mother on the loose, dreaming of a blueberry pie that's going to slay 'em. There, at the lake, they wear shorts, ankle socks, and sandals, and the most absurd straw hats they can find. And they never get tans.

As long as women have children, there will be moms. External customs and ways of life may change, but essentially moms never change. "A mother," says my mom, "is someone who has your interest at heart, for no other reason than that she loves you. There's no advantage to it, no prestige to it, it's just normal. She may not like the things you do, but she still loves you. And that's the thing that doesn't change."

In my generation, she was the mom who always wore an apron, who was up at the "crack of dawn", no matter how black or impossibly cold; who had the oatmeal porridge ready to stick to your ribs so that when she wrapped a scarf around your forehead, over your nose and mouth, tied it at the back, and sent you off, you had a good chance of making it to school. She was the mom who was there with chicken noodle soup and goulash when you came home at noon; who was there after four to answer the "mo-om" you hollered when you came in the front door; who listened again to how those boys threw snowballs at you on the way home from school, as she took one sheet of cookies from the oven and put another in, or iced a cake and left the bowl and spatula for you to lick; who was always there, year in and year out, at her place before the kitchen sink, which she'd occupied so habitually it had become her home, a space no one else claimed as she did, with its tunnels worn through the air to the stove and back to the sink, to the counter and back to the sink, to the dining room table, to the garbage can and back to the sink, aproned tummy bumping against the counter as she peeled the tons of potatoes and cut up the bushels of carrots, then set the pots on the stove to boil, instructing herself under her breath, "now I'll just make a salad and put the butter out and we're all set . . . ", building up to the moment Dad returned from The Office, doffed his toe rubbers at the back door, took the earmuffs from under his Homburg, slid his steamed-up glasses down his nose, and started in on his news too, until dinner was ready and she'd hoo-hoo to all within hearing distance, "I'm pudding gout'." A mom who filed everything under a personal system, known to the family but fully understood only by her, with one place for wooden spoons and another place for cookie cutters, places that became their homes, a home for the waxed paper, a home for the bread knives; the mom who had absolute power over all utensils, every knife and pot a familiar friend—"the one with the bent tip", "the one with the wooden handle"—with its own place in her private hierarchy of preference. The mom who put the leftovers in little Pyrex dishes and covered them with foil, with plans for all of them as she deposited them in the refrigerator; who polished taps and any visible chrome with a dry linen tea towel the moment they got spotty, and who dug around the burners with a paring knife to get the guck out so the stove looked cleaner. A mom whose main responsibility was the home and the children; who washed and ironed your clothes and always had a clean blouse for you; who changed your bed; who cleaned the house; who supervised your measles or chicken pox or whooping cough; who served you egg nog and glasses of warm milk in bed; who applied the mustard plaster and rubbed your chest with Vicks VapoRub; who shepherded you to the dentist, to the doctor, to ballet lessons, to swimming lessons; who painstakingly sewed you a ballerina's tutu out of peach-coloured crepe paper with an accordion-pleated skirt for the beach masquerade; who sewed you a costume for the skating carnival; who took you down to Eaton's on trips to buy you Savage shoes, when you could see your toes wiggling in the X-ray machine, or to buy you a new hat to wear to church on Easter Sunday, or who got totally involved in how you would look in your first strapless and first spike heels for the high school graduation dance; to whom you could always turn to listen to any problem; with whom there was always a chance for an appeal when pop laid down the law; who said nary a word about her own problems; who never asked anything of you while you asked the world of her; who was always there, for you, at home, at once the family menial and its symbolic heart; to whom its members related more strongly than they did to each other; upon whom their affection is projected, a force so powerful that without her there, at the centre, the symbol of harmony, security, understanding, and love, there would be no family. The mom you took for granted because she loved you; she who tucked you in and gave you a kiss good night.

My mom, Edith McCracken, is such a mom. She is 70 going on 24. Because she's a blonde and buxom, pretty one, with a youthful spirit, she's always given the impression of being much younger than she really is. Her eyes are pale blue, alert and understanding, her nose is small and straight, her face gently round and affectionate with cheeks that have always been naturally too rosy. She is a cuddly five feet four; unlike most women her age she continues to go in and out in the right places. Her bosom, or "bazoom", as she calls it, is large enough to require understatement. Her hips are trim—one is slightly larger than the other from carrying my brother around on it when he was a baby, and her legs are great. Her upper arms are the rolling pin kind, full of goodness and love, her forearms are strong and freckly, and her hands are small and vital; her pinky was stepped on by a playmate when she was little and is permanently crooked, perfect for holding teacups.

Although she's always looked the same, her hair and glasses have changed through the years. Now she wears her hair swept around in a gracious way in the back and short in the front, and her glasses are sophisticated, honorary-mother glasses with squarish mauve frames. She has always worn girdles, slips, nylons or pantyhose, under slacks too, and earrings. She likes simple dresses in bright colours or navy blue and white with hats to match. She never wore trousers till pantsuits came in, and still looks more at home in a dress, nylons, and high heels.

Although she looks the perfect lady, sitting on the flowered couch in the living room with her upswept hair, earrings, her trim, nyloned ankles crossed, balancing a teacup with a practiced hand, inside she's pretty nutty. When she gets the sillies, her face turns red, and girlish giggles squeeze out every pore until she gasps "Oh Dear" and wipes a tear from her eye. When I was little, she wore her hair up like Betty Grable, tied in a kerchief the way women in munitions plants during "The War" used to wear them. In an old shirt of my father's, pink pedal pushers, ankle socks, and "wedgies" she'd Charleston her way around the kitchen, making "froggy faces" or breaking into soulful renditions of "Because" or songs like:

"I know a girl called Sweet Hortense
 She ain't good lookin' but she's got good sense
 She's got lovely teeth in her mouth
 One points north and the other points south
 Gee, they're both immense
 You never saw a girl like Sweet Hortense."

My mom has always been a singer. There's lots of showgirl in her and she's often said she wished she could have sung with a band. If she'd lived in my generation, she might have been an Anne Murray, but because she grew up in a small prairie town in a Methodist family that went to church every Sunday, and because her own mother led the church choir for 19 years, her singing has been done mostly in church choirs. She used to perform as the soloist at weddings, in a hat, with her white gloved hands clasped under her bazoom, rolling her eyes on the high notes down to us kids. She led her own choir at Fort Garry United Church for ten years, and now sings in the choir at Augustine United Church. Going to church on Sunday means seeing mom up there in the choir loft, in her maroon surplice with the white dickie, singing her part from her score. She's gone to choir practice for one night a week for as long as I can remember; she used to practise her arpeggios in the kitchen while she was doing the baking and one time she was answered by a hoot from outside, the teen-aged boy next door mimicking her in falsetto.

It's hard to see your own mom as a person, because the biological closeness between you colours your view of her. To her friends, my mom is an individual personality who shares things in common with them, but to me, she is always mom. She had the same problem with her mom, too. "I would see my mother in a situation among her friends," says mom, "everybody calling her Vera and treating her as if she were just like they were. And she wasn't. Because she was mother. I always felt left out because I didn't know her that way."

I know my mom is a romantic. She loves Chopin and Strauss waltzes, and when something "sends" her, she clasps her hands together and exclaims spontaneously, "Oh, I love that!" She has written me letters almost weekly since I left home twelve years ago. In one of them, sent from the cottage, I found, "The weather is wonderful, and a night or two ago, I had to get up for you know what and looked out at the beauty outside there. Moonlight flooded the world! The trees, those three, stood silent and dignified. Everything seemed to be peaceful, and just breathless with the perfect night. It does something to one, and the question is, how does one respond to it, what can one do but enjoy? Full moon time is nice in the city, but out here it is moving!"

I think she's very intelligent, but since she hasn't had a career for over forty years she hasn't had any obvious way of proving it, nor has she developed the grim grey rationality of today's intelligent woman, probably because she's been pretty and protected. Her bubbly blondness actually conceals her intelligence, and being intelligent doesn't seem very important to her. But it's there, and it betrays itself in how quickly she picks up ideas, and how deeply she understands situations. She reads a lot and likes good literature, as well as whodunits, but she hasn't entered any of the traditional male arenas.

Because she's married to a businessman, who takes care of

the economic and political pole of reality, she is custodian of the humanistic pole of values. If being intelligent isn't that important to her, being loving is. She is strong, open, and deep; the things she says are very simple, but universally true. She loves people; she touches people when she talks to them and hugs them spontaneously. People are always individuals to her, the old and the sick people at the hospital where she works, or the wildest, hairiest hippy friend of mine she's met. Being young inside, she is always sympathetic to young people. I can remember, when I was in high school, having a gang of boys in baseball jackets and drapes over to play Ping-pong. I wondered where they'd all disappeared to, until I found them outside sitting on the grass talking to my mom. My mom's best friends now are young people. "I'm very fond of those girls," says mom. "They're young enough to be my daughters, but I still enjoy them very much. It's a matter of outlook. If you can identify with them and share the things that they share, age doesn't make any difference."

She lives by Christ's "Do Unto Others As You Would Have Them Do Unto You", which she calls "what y'gives y'gets", which she learned in childhood. She has often said that her purpose on earth must have been to make people happy, to be fun. She seems to have a glow that comes from inside, as if she's pink and gold all the way through. Her glow is so extraordinary, people remark on it. I asked her about it, and she said that people mention it to her, but it makes her self-conscious to think about it. Like the sun, my mother glows with positive energy, the life force, and I believe that the source of her glow is love.

My mom is an individual, but typical at the same time. She is the transition between pioneer and urban radical, between strict rural tradition and new freedoms. She became a housewife when the family was the unquestioned core of life, when men ruled the world, when sex and procreation went together, when childbearing was a woman's lot, when the work women did at home was real and economically necessary, when life was simple if you followed the Bible, based around marriage, the church, home, and family. Marriage vows were taken very seriously, as a consummation of the holy permanent bond essential to procreation, and marriage was the only course. A spinster was an object of ridicule. Families were large; since there was no sure way of stopping them, children could only be considered a blessing. The wife produced children for as long as she was fertile; a barren woman was tragic. Once you were married, you were safe, and a happy, prosperous life was assured.

As she moves into the twilight of her career, the family unit is disintegrating; people go in their own direction almost as often as they stick together, and women are deciding to bring up children by themselves. It is a time when sex and babies are two different things, when children in an over-populated world are a liability, not a blessing, when they grow up in day-care centres instead of at home, when spirituality is no longer the exclusive prerogative of the church, when social activism has taken the place of good works and when most people live in cities and have lost touch with the earth and the Bible.

Who are these mommas and what forces made them what they are today? If my mom is typical, her origins also are typical of her generation of mommas.

My mom's grandmother, Catherine Owen, married Thomas Harrison, in 1862. They had the usual large family, five boys and a girl, Vera, and owned a store in Thorndale, Ontario. They came west on the Canadian government's offer of land in the Homestead Act of 1882, when Thomas decided to buy land in the town of Neepawa, 25 or so miles west from the railroad line that ran south through Carberry and Brandon, in Manitoba and to homestead a farm out from there.

In 1886, the family moved lock, stock, and barrel to Neepawa. Thomas's land was on the Neepawa hill, at the corner of two gravel roads near the centre of town, about two blocks north of what is now Manitoba Number 4. The men put up a barn, and a house, a frame building with a mansard roof, which was ready to move into in the late fall of 1886. Thomas opened a lumberyard, and supplied the lumber for large houses with billiard rooms and drawing rooms with hardwood floors, for schools, for churches, for the Oddfellows Hall and the Opera House. He homesteaded a farm 8 or 9 miles south of Neepawa, but, as the lumberyard was doing very well and he didn't have time for both, he gave it up.

The Harrison family was active in the Methodist Church. The Harrison house had an organ that you pumped with your feet, with round stops you pulled out to adjust the tone. Vera took organ lessons and practised at home. Everyone in the family sang, Vera with a deep contralto. They all loved music, and Sunday nights after church, crowds would come together to sing hymns.

Vera came into Winnipeg to take her grade 12, then her Normal, one year of teacher's training. Along came a young man from New Brunswick to work in the general store in Neepawa. Jack Cochran was handsome, had a tremendous sense of fun and a high, clear tenor voice. They were married in November, 1902, and two years later, Edith Catherine Cochran, my mom, was born.

Bill Harrison, one of the Harrison boys, remained a bachelor, and stayed on in the Harrison house to become a partner in the lumberyard. On his suggestion, Jack opened a store in Winnipeg, while Vera stayed in Neepawa to take care of Edith. It was very hot the summer of 1905 and when Vera went in to Winnipeg, Jack was not well. There was no refrigeration, the flies were bad, perhaps the milk had become infected. Jack developed typhoid fever and died at 32. Widowed at 26, Vera became a recluse, and sat doing embroidery in her black dress, giving more and more of herself to the little girl. So Edith grew up in the Harrison home as a very cherished child, surrounded by adults. Her mom taught school at the Neepawa public school. She was an avid bridge player, led the Neepawa United Church choir, and recovered from her grief to regain her outgoing spirit and love of people. Later, on her summer vacations, she would get on the Greyhound bus at the bus depot across the street and travel alone everywhere. Grandma, Catherine Owen Harrison, lived on in the house until she died at 94, and Bill Harrison, known to my mother as Uncle Bill, lived on there too.

Uncle Bill was a searcher, sceptical of existing religions and of orthodox Christianity. He subscribed to "The Philistine", a contemporary radical magazine, and in it would get wind of books and order them by mail, mostly from the States. Edith watched Uncle Bill put up the book shelves, and helped him put in the sets of books when they arrived. Uncle Bill's library was the first room off the large front hall, a small dark room lined floor to ceiling on three sides with books—*Practical Yoga*, De Quincey's *Confessions of an English Opium Eater, The Waverley Novels*, the complete works of Edgar Allen Poe, Conan Doyle, Dickens, Carlyle, Ruskin, Tennyson, Darwin, Bunyan, Longfellow, Wordsworth, Coleridge, O. Henry, Joseph Conrad, Jack London, Rider Haggard, Ernest Thompson Seton, Shakespeare, and The *Books of Knowledge*.

Uncle Bill sat and read every night in the lugubrious light of a bronze Victorian lamp, until every book in his library was read, underlined, and equipped with several string bookmarks at significant pages. The great debate at the end of the nineteenth century was evolution versus creation, and books supporting both arguments rubbed covers in his library. Uncle Bill espoused evolution. "He put doubts in my mind about Christ being the son of God," says mother. " 'They can't prove that', he'd say. It had quite an impact on a girl of 16 or 17. Eva [her girlfriend] and I used to go way off in the back garden under a tree to talk about it because we were afraid to ask questions in front of God." Edith read most of the books too.

Uncle Bill was a great influence on her and sparked her interest in literature.

My mother remembers the house being very happy, full of music and activity, with Uncle Roy, a doctor and baseball fan, popping in at odd times, collapsing on the couch in the library and immediately snoring, and Uncle Bill trying to be a maestro on piano, violin, saxophone, and slide whistle. Edith sang in the church choir too, learned to play the violin and took piano lessons from Mrs. Cochran's teacher, practising on the old piano in the parlor. She learned every hymn by heart, and any place the hymn book fell open, she knew the words and the tune. Church was an integral part of her life, and Uncle Bill did not succeed in shaking the belief in Christianity instilled in her by Mrs. Cochran.

At that time, life in Neepawa was paradoxical. On the one hand, the ladies of the town each had visiting days, days on which their women friends would visit. They had calling cards which they left on a silver salver at the front door, so the hostess would know who had called, and would pay a return visit on the other women's "days". Tea was served in tiny delicate demi-tasse cups, and the ladies would sit in the parlor in their hats and long dresses, sipping tea and exchanging gossip. In contrast with such charming Victorian customs, life was still very close to nature. Wood was used to heat the house and to feed the fire in the big wood stove in the kitchen. "Cordwood-sized logs of oak and tamarack were sent sliding down a chute into the cellar, then piled up. The rest of the load was piled up beside the house ready for when the cellar was empty. It was a man-sized task to get a large oak log into the furnace. The sawing machine came around to cut the load of poplar wood into lengths for the stove. Then of course it had to be carried into the house. Usually, you picked up your armful on your way back from the backhouse."

The big house had no electricity. Gas lamps were installed in the front parlor and dining room, but were seldom used because of the risk of fire, so coal oil lamps were the only light. "I think I was about twelve years old when Uncle Bill had electricity installed in the house. I stood on a table in the kitchen and pulled on the first light. Great excitement!" Nor was there running water. "We used to go out to the backhouse with cape and cap and lantern on 40-below nights. The stuff froze and made a big pile, and we'd have to push it over to make room for more. Ugh! The slops from the kitchen—dishwater and washwater and some garbage—were carried out and thrown on the garden, so that by the end of February we had a brown bumpy ice lake. When the thaw came, because the house was at ground level, we had to keep sweeping the water away, and dig trenches to keep it from running in the back door."

There was an enormous amount of work in the house to be done to keep things going, done by the women, assisted by "hired help" in the Victorian tradition, hired girls who "lived in". "The washing day was exhausting! The boiler was filled and put on the stove with a cake of Sunlight or Fels Naptha soap sliced into it, on Sunday night. On Monday, Mrs. Radley came. The washing machine was hand run. Wet clothes were hung on clothes racks in winter, and placed over the registers, and sheets and shirts and heavy underwear hung in the pantry over bars which spanned the room from the top of one cupboard to the other. To get to the breadbox, you had to duck under long johns and flanelette sheets. The linen was not too gleaming white. All the water had to be carried out pail by pail, the soapy and then the blue rinse water, and thrown out on the garden lake. Then Mrs. Radley had her afternoon "cuppa" and was paid—a dollar? and shared the local gossip with Granma.

"Ironing was usually done on Tuesday. You ironed on a table covered with a blanket, then a sheet. The irons were flat irons with one detachable handle. The fire in the stove had to be consistently hot. The three irons were covered with a pan to make them heat faster. Then you used one until it was no longer warm enough, testing it with a wet finger, or spitting on it. Then you put that one back and took another. There was a characteristic sound that went along with ironing—the bang of the pan on the stove, the clink of the iron on the ironstand while you turned your article, the creak of the kitchen table as you worked, and always the smell of clean clothes and hot scorched paper, because you tested your iron on the *Neepawa Press* or *The Winnipeg Telegram*."

When she was 16, the blossoming young Edith Cochran went in to Winnipeg to attend Wesley College on Portage Avenue, now United College. She graduated in 1924, and went to Normal, as her mother had done. But instead of going back to Neepawa to teach, she spent four years teaching in small prairie towns—Gilbert Plains, Swan River, and Dauphin. "I lived in a boarding place and went home for lunch. There wasn't much social activity. I wasn't a good teacher, and I didn't like teaching because I wasn't a successful teacher. I felt I wasn't doing a good job. You were supposed to stick to the program. At 3:30 on Friday afternoons, you were supposed to be doing health, and they'd come around and check to make sure you were doing health." She earned a monthly salary of $160 in Dauphin.

So my mom had her career. "You were supposed to have had your freedom before you were married, but you knew all along what you were going to do." At the boarding house, she met another schoolteacher, Bill McCracken, from Moosomin, Saskatchewan. He was a good tennis player, wore white linen trousers, was tall and dark, in the thin moustache of the times, and was funny and clever. He was coming in to Winnipeg and Edith decided coincidentally that she would come into Winnipeg to take singing lessons. She taught in Winnipeg for three years, and took several choirs into the Manitoba Music Festival, which began in 1919. She still had musical ambitions. "Did I want to be a song and dance girl? You betcha! In college I did stunt night things. Each year would present an item. I did 'In my Sweet Little Alice Blue Gown' in a paper dress and sang in an operetta as Princess someone or other. My singing teacher said I could have done musical comedy. But I didn't have the push or the connections, and I had a man who wanted to marry me." So Edith Cochran and Bill McCracken were married in Neepawa in 1932. Mrs. Cochran and Uncle Bill passed on in the Fifties and the Harrison house was sold to the garage next door in 1959. Where the house stood now are gas pumps and where the barn was, the Neepawa Post Office now stands.

During the Depression, according to mom, married women supported by a husband weren't supposed to work. If a woman had a working husband, she couldn't take a job, because she might take that job away from the father of a family. Jobs were to keep you alive; you worked to eat not because you enjoyed it. Women who were doctors, she admits, probably kept on working, but the ambition of most women was to get married, and when they did, they usually quit their jobs. Being supported by a man looked more attractive to women than it does today. "I was bloody damn well glad to get out of my career," she says. "If it had been something I really *liked* doing, interior decorating, nutrition, or home economy, I would have been reluctant to give it over. I would have been good at those things."

They lived in an apartment in Winnipeg. She had a cat; they went back and forth to Neepawa; they made furniture; she dyed curtains; they had fun with the neighbours; and she practised "Jesu Joy of Man's Desiring" on the piano, and learned to play "The Minute Waltz" in five minutes. She didn't like living in an apartment. "There was no place to go outside. You couldn't even shake a mop." They found a house in Fort Garry, which they could have free for three months, if they cleaned it up, and they did that, which was fun. Like any young couple in the Depression, they had a hard time making ends meet. To spend a quarter going to the picture show required deliberation. Mrs. Cochran would send mom five dollars and laugh at how she managed to spend it fourteen different ways. She soon developed a quirk about making things last. Cuffs on shirts were turned, socks were darned, leftovers all used up. "You didn't splurge on anything," she says. She still has this quirk. She saves pieces of foil, to be used over again. She says that when plastic bags first came out, a woman she knew had her kitchen draped with clotheslines, with plastic bags washed out and pinned up with clothespins to dry.

After she was married, her attention turned to making a home, with her husband. A wife was not considered someone whose career would be housework, while her husband had his career in the outside world. What they were doing was building a home together, and part of that was doing housework. My mom, after her teaching experience, didn't particularly want children. "Children are fine one at a time," she said, "Not in screaming classrooms of grade nines." So she and father were free until I arrived eight years later, and then the housework began in earnest, as children, not marriage create housework. My mom did the same things as had been done in the house in Neepawa, the washing, ironing, cleaning, cooking, and baking—but in newer ways.

She spent Mondays in the basement, wrestling with an ancient mechanical square washing machine that cost $5. The water in it had to be emptied by hand using galvanized steel tubs, the wringer turned with a crank. She won an electric refrigerator in a General Electric essay contest; the topic was "I Live Better Electrically Because . . . " It was a real advance when she got an electric wringer washer that pumped its own water into the basement sink. A Westinghouse, I think it was—I can remember her telling me a story about a wabbit who wived in a Westinghouse.

Sometimes I helped her with the blueing. Little nuggets of

blue pool-cue chalk were sold wrapped in pieces of cotton tied with string. You rinsed the sheets in cold water with the blueing, and then had to rescue the much-diminished piece of blueing from the icy water. Mom starched shirt collars and cuffs by soaking them in cornstarch diluted with water. She put the washing in a wicker basket, carted it upstairs, and hung it on the line. On Mondays, washings all down the street would be flapping in the wind, and when the wind blew the wrong way, fly-ash from the smokestacks of steam engines would land on the clean sheets, dealing the struggle for whiteness a mortal blow. And in Winnipeg, where it gets so cold the trees crack like rifles, she'd hang the things that wouldn't fit in the basement outside. They'd freeze, and she'd bring in sheets that stood up like boards.

She then had to iron all the clothes she'd washed. She did them all by herself, standing at a wooden ironing board with an iron that was electric but wasn't a steam iron, so she'd have to first spend a while dampening, sprinkling water on the clothes with her hand or with a Coke bottle fitted with a sprinkle cap, and roll them up in bundles. A father required a clean shirt almost every day, since a dirty shirt or a frayed shirt collar might affect the impression he made at the office.

She did most of the housecleaning, although she did have cleaning ladies and sometimes cleaning men. She'd scrub the kitchen floor with a scrubbing brush and pail, and wax the hardwood floors by hand. Then she'd polish them by rubbing a contraption that consisted of a lead weight on the end of a broom handle, placed on a soft cloth, back and forth over the floor. She mopped and shook the mop out the back door, in the classic housewife's gesture immortalized by cartoonists.

She did the baking; she made pies, cakes, cookies, nuts, breads, baking powder biscuits, scones, oatmeal, chocolate chip, shortbread, and peanut butter cookies, not just once to see how they came out, but over and over regularly, to keep a supply that would survive my brother's and my relentless raiding of the cookie tin. Did our gusto for goodies tyrannize my mom into keeping a constant supply flowing out from under her floury hands, or did she do it because she liked seeing us gobble them up? Whatever, she did it, providing breakfasts, lunches, and the evening meal.

Being a mom was a full time job. Not only did she stay home and do all this, but when her children were small, she had to deal with cloth diapers, rinsing them, soaking them, bleaching them, to always have a sterile supply on hand. She made her own formula, and sterilized the bottles. She washed and ironed baby clothes, and made little dresses with smocking and puffy sleeves by hand for me.

When she started, and money was tight, the work she did in the house was economically necessary and contributed a good deal to a high standard of family well-being. A wife had her end to hold up. Housewives were oppressed; the tools of her trade—the scrubbing brush, ironing board, mixing bowls, and cake tins—bound her like chains to her choice. But family survival was at stake; the economic margins and individual freedom of today didn't exist. The wife was part of the family unit, and this was her work. Weeks, months, and years rolled by as mom stood in her apron by the sink peeling the potatoes, the carrots, turning out cookies, and cakes, and pies for the family and dainties for hospital, church, and school teas, and doing thousands of washings, and ironings, and housecleanings.

Slowly the children grew, and slowly the financial situation improved; she continued to do the same things, except that the equipment she did them with improved, too. Part of the fun was deciding with pop about which of the post-war blessings of American technology to buy, and these made her work easier. An automatic washer and dryer, a steam iron, a dishwasher, a freezer, a pop-up toaster, an electric mixer, an electric kettle, a tile kitchen floor, wall-to-wall carpet. These advances meant a lot to people of my parents' generation because they know what life was like without them, and such "labour-saving devices" actually did save a lot of work. Other advances came along—nylon, orlon, terylene, drip dry, wash'n wear, no iron, permanent press, cake mixes, instant pie crust, frozen foods, instant coffee, aerosol cans of window cleaner, and oven cleaner—which continued to simplify her work. But her life—her husband, her children, her friends, the church, the choir, bridge, golf, curling, reading, and music—remained the same.

Technology may almost have done her out of a job, but it hasn't done my mother out of her role. She likes her role. She gets up early in the morning, in a good mood. She likes to be active, and she assumes responsibility so naturally that you hardly notice that before you've had a chance to wash your dishes, she's washed them, before you've thought of putting your clothes in the washer, she's done it. She enjoys it because she's productive and because she does it herself. And, being the expert she can do things faster than anyone else, and it makes her feel good.

She still prepares a big meal every night, which isn't easy. Sometimes she outdoes herself with a Cornish game hen spectacular, but as often as not, she simply whips some ground meat and stewed tomatoes together, but because it's she who's done it it comes off as a major production. Sometimes, she doesn't feel like cooking, and looking at everybody sitting around moaning about how hungry they are, she knows that she's expected to cook and wonders what she's got herself into. I can't make the dinner in her place. Ever since the gazpacho and the Chicken Kiev, nobody trusts my cooking. I don't have the right touch. When I offer to help, she declines. The only thing she'll get me to do is peel the occasional vegetable, set the table or make the salad.

On hot summer days at the lake, when the water is shimmering and beckoning blue and gold, where is she but in the kitchen, whomping up a blueberry pie or oatmeal cookies.

She makes cakes for recreation. She doesn't force people to eat; instead she seduces them with fresh strawberries, angel food cake, whipped cream, and mouth-watering pies. I don't eat sweets much, but when I'm visiting at home, I'm in there gobbling up with the best of them. She cooks with love. And if there's a secret to her survival as a housewife and an individual, it's that she has seen being a good housewife and mother as a challenge to her virtue; she is so generous, loving, and understanding, and so quick to see things that need to be done, that like a white tornado she simply outdoes everyone else.

On a summer night a few years ago at the cottage, mom licked me at Scrabble, as she does occasionally. Anyone who loses a Scrabble game feels a little put down and I did then, especially since I was the career type, a professional writer at that, and she was just a housewife who wasn't supposed to be that smart. She went over and sat down on the sofa. A look passed between us that wasn't a mother-daughter look, but a kind of query that said, "Here we are in the same place at the same time, but we have made different choices. Why are we so different?"

There are complicated reasons for the differences. Many of them have to do with my mother. She got married. She had an ego, but she didn't fulfill it in a career. She listened to the radio, and her ego told her that she could sing as well as the people singing on it, and one day she did tuck some sheet music under her arm and go down and audition—but she got scared and took her ego home and buried it behind the garage. So she simply never knew how far she could have gone.

She put all kinds of energy into me. I never stood in her place in the kitchen once when I was growing up. Instead, I hung around the edges, telling her my problems, licking icing dishes and feeling guilty for letting her do all the work. I sat outside in the sun reading in my bathing suit while she bustled around the kitchen. She listened to me search my soul till she was blue in the face; the dynamic of conversation between us was usually that I was talking about myself and she was talking about me, too. I watched her in her housebound position, picking up and putting away in what she calls Toujours le Putaway, and I felt I didn't want to be in that position myself. I found it hard to understand what such a talented, pretty, and intelligent woman was doing scrubbing floors; surely, I thought, she could have done something in the world. Her selflessness and generosity towards me created in me the egotism it took to go out in the world and do something. I was the missing piece, the ego, returned from behind the garage. Like her mother, she wanted me to be a ballet dancer too; so did I, but I flunked the first exam by hoping a squat would pass for a plié. I cast around for something to do; I wanted to be a painter, but I was stronger in literature, possibly because of her support at home. But as she supported my dad and my brother, she supported me. My ego was the caryatid and she was the pedestal that supported it. In today's language, that means I was one of her oppressors. But did she consider it an oppression? At times, perhaps, but it was her choice, and she accepted it.

I identified with the generation that broke with tradition. Many of us don't play bridge, sing in church choirs, or go to church. We shun material possessions; our progression is supposed to have been spiritual rather than material. We don't do charity work, we are community activists. We drink. We make love without being married and without having babies. We ride bicycles, and eat health food. But sometimes it appears we are doing the same things as our parents did on a different level, and life may turn us into our parents, with minor modifications.

Life is longer and slower than we sometimes realize. My mom has been through two wars and a depression, the births of two children and the deaths of her and my father's parents. She was a girl, she was beautiful, she had boyfriends, and she worked out in the world. But I didn't know her as that person.

By the time I knew her, she was over 40, an age I haven't reached yet, and a housewife and mother. Just because she didn't have a lifelong external career, and stayed home and did housework, does that mean she's not a person? You might just as well say that I am not a person because I am not married.

Far from being a non-person, my mother is a wonderful person. She is not hard, but she is strong. Strength is a softer, more inward and tolerant quality that rolls with the punches; hardness is brittle and breaks. She has a lot of courage too. She is a religious person at heart and knows the importance of love and that the secret of life is heart. She is ready to be blamed by an immature child who hasn't yet the courage to admit that her mistakes are her own. She accepts responsibility for her own mistakes. She simply lives all situations through being as positive as possible throughout. She is very wise. You can learn an awful lot from your mom. And I think her values are good for all time.

My mom is very much like her mother, and as she grows older and more dignified, the resemblance increases. Mrs. Cochran's features are there in her smile, in the way her skirt falls around her well-shaped legs when she bends over to pick something up, in her quick hands, and Mrs. Cochran's traditions—singing in the choir, playing bridge, doing crosswords and cryptograms, and caring about people—live on in my mom. When I look in the mirror now, I can see my mother's features behind my own. The same rounded cheeks, although mine have never been rosy. And something around the eyes, in a straight serious gaze, and in the upper lip, that is common to all three generations. I dance around the kitchen, I break out into French, I am musical, I like books and cooking. Perhaps when I am 70, I will be my mother too, in spite of everything. If I'm lucky.

Kathleen:
Amazon Daughter

BY MYRNA KOSTASH

I'm a demanding person. I demand a lot not only of
myself but of my friends, of society. I demand everything
I can get, every potential I have. I became a feminist when
I realized I wasn't getting what I wanted because I am a
woman. If Women's Liberation hadn't been around, I
would have invented it.

In her twenty-first year, this much can be said about
Kathleen: she is short, slender, blonde, and has a raspy voice;
before she came to the university she had experimented with
drugs, messed with sex, coped with poverty, and endured
homelessness; she is now studying to be a lawyer; she can flip
a man over her shoulder; she has an ego like the Rock of
Gibraltar. She is a feminist. I want to know how she got there
and what she means by the word. I want to know how the two
of us, eight years apart, ended up in the same ideology at the
same time. I want to know how she grew up at the tailend of
a decade in which I was a teen-ager, grew up and steered my
way unsteadily to end, in 1973, as an instructor in Women's
Studies, with a student called Kathleen.

Only eight years. Yet they mean she has a singular tough-
ness, that quality of defiance mixed with shrewdness which
distinguishes her so remarkably from the twenty-year-olds I
and my friends were, when we were soft and timid creatures,
bruised and confounded by the apparent cruelty and careless-
ness of the masculine world to which we bared our sacrificial

bodies and spirits, thinking that was what was required if we were to be loved. I remember, like snapshots, those wounded, hopeful mid-Sixties female faces that have closed over now into masks for women who are disciplining children and reading *Ms* magazine. Kathleen, of course, will have none of that. Even while she messed around, as we did, with cheap thrills and daring explorations, she knew who she was serving: herself. Where I and my friends drove ourselves with self-contempt, Kathleen was sure she was something special. And where we, out of all that, put together Women's Liberation, she has inherited it.

> Both my grandmother and mother run their families. Although my father is better educated and better read, he isn't interested in the down-to-earth realities of daily living. His mind and attention are somewhere else, on little strangenesses, so my mother's word goes on everything, not just on family and domestic stuff but even on what my father does and how. He doesn't mind, he prefers it that way. Both these women are stronger and more aggressive than their men. My father will get walked over by anybody. It's my mother who has to go ask for decent wages from his employer. Yet she always says it's his word that goes. All through my childhood I had thought my father was the head of the family.

Her Irish father is a jazz musician, a carpenter, a drinker, a sentimentalist, a patriot, a mystic. Her Irish mother has borne ten children, instructed them in basics, and left them to grow up as well as they may. Kathleen was born, slight and fair, in Connaught, Ireland, on the sea coast, in December, 1952. Five years later, Kathleen and her family had moved to Toronto. But still she is Irish. The family patriarchs were officer-grandfathers in the IRA, one who blew up British ships, another who tried to kill Lloyd George and who beat his tiny wife—he was often drunk. Their son, her father, who has never raised himself in violence against *his* wife, Kathleen's mother, wept upon reading an Irish novel in which men beat women ("I would never marry an Irishman," says Kathleen). As for matriarchs, there were two grandmothers, the tiny one, who tried to abort herself and failed, another who has never cooked or cleaned house in all her life but who bore, anyway, fourteen children and delivered rifles hidden under blankets in a pram to the IRA.

The matriarchal figure, or, rather, the image of the Mother emerges in this case, from a marriage in which the father declined the role and the mother assumed it by some other name. In a family of eight daughters, this is important—to Kathleen at least, who has never admired "little girls". Instead, she allied with her mother's strength; "in times of panic, you know, hard times, financial crises, she will not break down, she will not fall apart." And when she says this I think of Rose Anna Lacasse in *The Tin Flute* and Gertrude Morel in *Sons and Lovers* and of Maria Chapdelaine, too, who were required by the material conditions of their lives to *hang in there*, to balance the needs and undeniable demands of the belly and the nervous system with those of the heart, and when it all unbalanced, to patch things up, mend the tears and—this is important—never to complain. While the patriarchs flail about in existential anguishes, Mother will heal us all when we come back scarred and scared, with chicken soup and a big milky bosom.

Yes, such women are important for daughters. Not only as a model for survival and endurance but also as the propagandist for another way of life altogether—" 'little one, you don't have to live like this.' My mother was heart-broken when my sisters married, one of them at eighteen. She doesn't want us to get married and have children. She once said that of course she isn't sorry that any of us were born but at times she is sorry she had so many—her pregnancies were so regular nobody took any notice of them—but that, in the end, what else was she to do, given who she was, a poor, ill-educated Irish Catholic girl? And she believes now that it was her one exceptional act, having brought up ten 'brilliant' children. But it's different for us. She wants us to do things in life." There's pregnancy, mothering, housewifery, on the one hand. There's Kathleen's future on the other.

But the household was happy and healthy for all that, for all the unemployment, and houses with cockroaches, the move from street to street, the tempers and stubbornesses. A satisfying place in spite of the father's timidity and lost dreams, the mother's worries, their disputes and struggles (never in front of the children) at the local pub, the troubles with landlords and evictions, and the family superstitions, the conviction that houses are haunted and that spirits and dead souls inhabit inanimate things. Kathleen grew up happily, madcap: "We always felt independent of our parents, we were left to grow up on our own, we were raised in a haphazard way", grew up to be her parents' good friend, getting drunk together, exchanging views. The house was always full of people having parties, drinking, singing, and playing Irish music, with a salute to the IRA revolutionary heroes in frames along the wall: "in financial crises we drink at home, other things are given up at those times but not the drinking, oh yeah, we all get drunk (laughs), last week my mother put on big construction boots and sang 'Knees Up Mother Brown'."

No conventional piety here, either, even though the children were sent to Mass and to parochial schools. A plastic statuette of St. Jude, patron saint of lost causes, sat on the television set until it was broken and never replaced, and a few times they tried a "family rosary", all on their knees in rows until the snickering got too loud and disrespectful, for her father is a self-proclaimed atheist who hated fish on Fridays and her mother was driven to the Confessional only at critical moments of her life, as when she had started to use the pill.

In other, different households, there are girls who grow up

girlish, in crinolines and pincurls, their mouths puckered coyly, sitting, ankles crossed, in front of the living room window, daddy's girl, am I pretty? There are others, like Kathleen, outside on the street in a pack of ethnic punk-kids, letting the air out of the tires of the neighbour's car.

It's important that I came from the working class. There simply wasn't the money for a girlish socialization, for the ruffly dresses, the dolls, the dancing lessons, and my mother didn't have the time to supervise and worry about me. So I was out in the streets with boys playing rough in t-shirts and jeans. And there wasn't money for that terrible thing that middle-class parents do to girls: send them to psychiatrists. Just as long as I was doing well in school and keeping out of trouble, my parents did not worry what was happening to my mind. If we were cheeky or sulky, they'd wallop us. They wouldn't think we were *sick*.

Kathleen was simply a girl-child, wore dresses and, along with her brothers, was told to observe good manners and not to swear. She never played with dolls, and doesn't remember ever having daydreamed about being a wife and mother. But she does remember daydreaming about being a pirate, having magical powers to fly and to walk through mirrors, being with Gene Autry, riding horses. And about wanting, later, to be an archaeologist, anthropologist, marine biologist, scuba diver. She read *The Girl's Own Annual* and stories about girl doctors and girl pilots; small wonder, that the ambitions of nurse and stewardess struck her as intolerably mediocre. She knew she had energy, wit, and grace, and she knew there would be some future worthy of them, something that broke through the ego limits of self-sacrificing, devotional women's work. In the meantime, at age eight, she started Irish dancing lessons which meant that, besides acquiring instruction in Irish folk arts, she gained some independence and learned about competition.

The dancers travelled to the States and to Ireland to compete in festivals and she early discovered she could take care of herself—and that she could win. She won thirty-one trophies in ten years, at festivals where the money taken in was sent to the IRA to buy guns: "I liked winning."

She followed a group of Irish kids from Regent Park (a public housing area in Toronto) into the Mischief Club. One member, a "big, tough girlfriend", was her bodyguard, and they played out in the streets, throwing stones through windows, over-turning garbage cans, and beating up Jehovah's Witnesses' kids. "We felt more adventurous than mischievous, we were bored . . . most of what we did was my idea." She was no lady at school, either. She was a good student but to her parents, who never knew about the Mischief Club, it was more important that she do well in Conduct than in Math. Still, she competed with gusto with her sisters ("I wanted to be brighter, more active than them all"), and spent several years learning to settle down. "I was always talking, eating candy, passing notes, tapping my feet under the desk, playing on the boys' side of the yard, dashing out to the bathroom without raising my hand first, and getting the strap because I wouldn't sit on my hands for as long as I was supposed to."

Somehow, in that boisterous Irish family, among the phantoms, shady warriors, drink, and lamentation, in the working-class streets, scrapes and childish wickedness, in the shadow of a barely-realized faith and in her own, ambitious fantasies, she was never really a Girl. Glory be, she had made a detour around the routes of femininity.

She had no clear idea, then, that there was a significant difference between girls and boys. Sure, the genitals were different. "As children, we got bathed together but, of course, since the girls outnumbered the boys five to one, it was my brothers who were abnormal, as far as we were concerned. The whole idea of 'penis envy' really makes me laugh." Her parents, and her teachers, never left her with the impression that she had a separate destiny to fulfill, pudenda-shaped, nor special privileges to expect, ladylike. According to her mother, she was to avoid husband and children; according to her father, she was to quit school at grade twelve and go working, to help the family out. If she didn't work, she was to leave their house. It was very simple. Male and female, you obeyed your parents, you paid your way and kept out of trouble. There were to be no exemptions from real life.

Well, there was one. You could become a nun. And, right up to grade ten, Kathleen wanted to be a nun. What is it about nuns, the figures floating along the sidewalk in long black skirts, the cross pressed against the starched white breast, the wan face peering out from a modest hood, so unutterably virginal?

But it was another kind of nun, Audrey Hepburn in a jungle hospital, that Kathleen admired. She wanted to be a missionary nun, one who would travel abroad and get things done; and for the longest time it seemed that only nuns could do it, all other women being held in thrall by fathers, lovers, and husbands. Nuns were special people, they lived close together and protected each other in an apparently friendly, peaceable community, with no men around. She would watch them walking together around the beautiful grounds of the convent, an island of green in this working-class district, and she wanted to grow old like that, supported by this benevolent sisterhood against the terrors of death.

As it turned out, however, she left the Church before any of that dream could happen. But the memory of these women is still sweet to her and she is grateful for the instruction they gave her:

I'm very very glad to have gone to an all-girls' high school. You don't waste time trying to attract boys, pretending you're dumb, overwhelmed by them, being ignored by teachers who would rather encourage the boys. Instead you have women teachers who encourage you, you learn to talk and debate with equals. One nun told us, 'I hope you girls realize that before you become wives and mothers you do have a duty towards society'. That's kind of a warped way of putting it, but still it was an encouragement. To get into the world and do something in it. I learned confidence from them in an atmosphere where we could compete and excel, all those things reserved for boys in co-ed schooling. All through school I had no real idea that being a female made me different from people. I saw women in control, with power—at home, at school, at dancing class—and I spent most of my time around women.

Perhaps that's what it is about nuns. Perhaps that's what it is about the nunnery.

As schoolgirls, my girlfriend and I made a pact in which we swore we would never allow a man to break up our friendship. I guess the pact came from the fear of having a boyfriend and later of losing our virginity. We had the distinct feeling that in whatever it is that happens between men and women, we were going to lose something, a part of what we were. We were fighting against the loss of our future.

In 1968, in east central Toronto, Kathleen was a teen-ager. Not anything like the one I was, in 1958, but someone closer to the mythologies of the Sixties in which I and my friends became grown-ups intoning holiness, good works, and salvation within the bogus shelters of hippy beatitude and campus liberation. Kathleen and her friends were refashioning the scraps and tatters of this into a cynical, hard-nosed, punk version of our woebegone naiveté. We had said we wanted peace and communism. *She* wanted, simply, experience, good times, and membership in an interesting gang. She went after them and got them, travelling at cosmic speed from absolute innocence, ignorance, and naiveté, to a life of weekend wickedness. And, unlike me, who had tripped over adolescence like a girl in daddy's shoes, she never missed a step. From smoking cigarettes at the back of the bus, and learning to neck, smooch smooch at the back of the bus, and discussing the technique with a girlfriend, from that sort of familiar naughtiness to this:

> I had a girlfriend, Gina, who went to a tough, ethnic, working-class school, her gang was into glue sniffing, dope, drinking, dropping acid since they were fourteen years old; one of them was supposedly connected with the Mafia as a dealer. Gina had lost her virginity at fourteen, and had been doing dope, was a high school band groupie. The boys in the group were older, like eighteen and nineteen, speed freaks, had parties that got raided. Anyway, I met Gina at a party and two guys, Ken and Tom walked in, obviously more experienced, long hair, and I wanted to belong to a peer group like this, more worldly. I thought these guys were just IT, they came in with two older girls, they smoked a joint. Up to then I had believed grass was an escape from reality, I used to lecture a friend of mine who would come to school stoned, I said hippies were ruining society, I defended the Vietnam war and said protests didn't accomplish anything. And these two guys, men of the world, obviously knew something different. They went into the bedroom with their girls and necked for an hour, which really impressed me. I thought they were very attractive, and their girlfriends seemed superior to me, so after the party I decided I wanted to be in their group. I changed my whole style of dress, wore really tight blue jeans, tight tops, wore my hair dead straight, lots of make-up, then I started going out with Tom, who was a real dope.

All my boyfriends have been dopes; I used to be proud

to say they were for fun and pleasure, and all my intellectual interests I shared with girls, just like a male chauvinist in reverse. I still don't like discussing politics and books with guys. Every time I've tried, I find I spend more time fighting for my right to hold an opinion than talking about what those opinions are, never equals in a discussion, never taken seriously, so I would go to girlfriends to talk intellectually about things that were important and close to me. I wasn't out to attract the whole male sex, I just wanted one boyfriend and once I had that, I didn't care about the rest of them. I never had crushes, never fell in love, never had love problems, a boyfriend was just something I had to have at my age.

Well, the deadpan of that delivery is staggering. I mean, at her age I was sleeping with rollers in my hair, begging my parents for money for a school sweater, and covering my mouth at the end of a date so I wouldn't get kissed. Her *sang-froid*, that way she had of moving in and out of a scene like a tourist taking photographs, her deliberate cultivation of experiences, by her own choice and desire instead of falling, as I did, willy-nilly, into whatever escapade offered itself (and which I could find no way of resisting), her *talent* for picking up whatever she wanted, unscathed, with minimal abuse to her ego while mine lay in shreds from the least rejection (the difference between taking and being taken), her lack of passion—all of it staggers me. It's not what I thought girls were like. Boys, yes, with their studied cool—"Baby, you're a drag"—and their excessive concern for an idiotic freedom—"Baby, don't get hung up on me"—but girls as I knew them, as we were, were bleating, bleeding lambs, "Do with me what you will, ba-a-a." And her way with the men would have been unimaginable to me: how on earth to think them unimportant, as outside my real concern and passion, when everything in my mind and heart revolved around their finding me lovable. Where did Kathleen find the courage to see them otherwise? In female friendship, perhaps; supportive, honest, affectionate. Perhaps in self-love, and the need to leave her mark in the world, fearing even then the bog of a love in which women work as coolies. Or perhaps in the turnaround of the survivor—it's either him or me—and since it's women who go mad, she would play the man's game of indifference.

Whatever it was, I was twenty-one and blubbering, she was sixteen and cool. Other differences are significant too: the working-class milieu, the petty crime, the heroin. They bespeak a struggle I never, in pleasant, middle-class Edmonton, had to take seriously, survival, and an attitude I would never have to assume, nihilism. Although Kathleen knew she wasn't going to get stuck, for the others there were few important alternatives to getting stoned, far away from droning schoolteachers and employers, and getting laid, free from the hassle of courtship. Kathleen and her friends didn't play at the edge, they *lived* there. What they were doing wasn't just for thrills, they knew it was the only way out of their parents' lives.

In the spring of 1970, Kathleen graduated from grade twelve, went to Ireland for the summer and never saw the east end crowd again. In the fall, she started work as a file clerk at Ontario Hydro. Her heart was set on going to university some day, but no child of her parents had ever been provided with a higher education; a *job* was more important. And at work, blowing her money on boots and midi skirts, bored among the file cabinets, arguing with co-workers about the sexual double standard, resenting having to make coffee for an office of men, some of whom were lower in status than she, and being told by her female supervisor, "For heaven's sake, Kathleen, wear a bra", she started to become a feminist. She settled the coffee problem by telling the men (she had just finished reading Tom Wolfe's *The Electric Kool-Aid Acid Test*) that she had doused their sugar cubes with LSD, and they believed her. She handled her resentment of her parents' failure to support her in grade thirteen, and thence to university, by moving out of their home. ("Well," they would say, "you realize you're not welcome in this house any more; we don't want to see you again.") She quit work before they could fire her, the day they found inside her desk some newspaper clippings and pro-abortion slogans that had been prepared for a demonstration: "Abort this government!" and "This chick follows no cock!"

She moved from house to house, finally settling in a commune of four men. She had only a closet of a room, but it was all *hers*, where she was looking after herself, making her own decisions, finding out, she says, who she was, in fact. A bonus: finally she was able to feel persecuted by parents, just as all her peers had been complaining for years. It was some kind of growing up.

> I didn't much care what his feelings were, not even his jealousy when I messed around with some of the other guys at parties when Tom would pass out, stoned. I would never for an instant have considered these guys my friends. Tom was turned on by my innocence, interested in virgin-stomping. I discovered later that I had much exaggerated his worldliness, actually I liked Ken better, but he wouldn't have anything to do with virgins. Tom fell in love with me, I think, would pat me on the head and call me 'little one'.
>
> The parties were very wild, everyone blind drunk, pushing people out of windows—we were on the fourth floor. These kids come from the lower working-class, from 'broken' homes, reformatories, their school has the reputation of being the biggest dope school in the city. We smoked grass and hash at the parties. It never occurred to me at the time that I would lose my virginity. I had my image as the innocent girl exploring varieties of experience, and people believed or respected that. It isn't that I wasn't ready for sex, I was just too chicken, I didn't know anything about birth control, we did everything but fuck,

I was just so glad to have a steady boyfriend. I sort of enjoyed it, but I was doing it really just to maintain my position in the group.

It certainly wasn't cool to freak out on acid, you had to keep the image, you couldn't even go to your boyfriend for help, in fact, chicks weren't supposed to take acid, they couldn't handle it. I took it, anyway, but I was told I wouldn't get help if I freaked out. This put me one up on Gina who had been one up on me because she wasn't a virgin and because she was hung-up on a hopeless case, Ken, who scored chicks everywhere. These people were also into stealing stereos and cameras from apartments and into speed. When I first took acid it was just a stone, I didn't learn to have revelations until later, just a stone with some interesting hallucinations and distortions. We had lots of music, we necked and screwed around, sat around having stoned conversations, danced. Two black guys taught everybody else how to dance, they also got into knife fights. I wanted to get into skin-popping junk but I was told that wasn't for girls either.

I had a double life, all week I was an exemplary student at St. Joan's School, I was a member of all the clubs, on the Student Council, a cheerleader, and that's what kept the weekend stuff a game, knowing I would never end up that way, just playing with it. I never told my boyfriends about my academic success, I didn't want them to know I was bright, it was all right for the boys, even the working-class ones, to do well at school, but not for girls. On weekends I would pack a bag and go stay with Gina; my parents didn't suspect a thing. Gina was a strange girl, the original flower child, who got badly used by the guys, gang bangs, and I never tried to help her, I thought it was her fault for letting herself be taken, ripped-off.

We had nothing to do with politics, although I remember getting into arguments about Women's Liberation. I would never back down on my position, although it wouldn't upset me either that people didn't take me seriously. Gina didn't believe in it at all. I would say I was a feminist, then I would laugh and say I wasn't really, and then the guys would pat me and say it was a good thing I knew my place, and then I would say, hey, that's not what I meant at all. I had pasted on my bedroom walls all the newspaper reports coming out about the Royal Commission on the Status of Women but, all in all, it wasn't a particularly intellectual period for me, I remember being bothered by the fact I was considered flat-chested.

The break had been made from one culture—the family, domestic continuity, daughter identity—but the new one she moved into did not, in the end, satisfy her. For sure it was good times, though, in that crazy household, lying on the floor with a stereo speaker at each ear, Bob Dylan, Pink Floyd, Frank Zappa, kaboom, kaboom, hoping that out of the stew of drugs in her brain (she would come home from work in a store and eat acid for supper), out of the tatterdemalion costumes draped over her body and the psychedelic posters on the wall and the shrine to Jimi Hendrix and Janis Joplin in the corner, out of the people who hung around—Larry who walked around nude, Chris with blond hair down to his waist, Janet and Sally, who worked as a team in bed with musicians—out of it would come the Revelation, a penetrating insight into the ways of things, just like the ones she'd read about in mystical texts. Why couldn't she have a Revelation too, or was she born rather too late for that sort of thing, had it self-destructed before her time, somewhere between *Highway 61 Revisited* and the assassination of Bobby Kennedy? "Romanticism was come and gone by the time the drug wave hit my generation. We were no longer calling each other beautiful, our trip was to turn ourselves from well-adjusted middle-class kids into filthy, dirty junkies."

Cynical as hell, these kids, the curl of the lip at a suggestion from those who had made the trip five years earlier that the point of such anarchic exercises, the heavy rock, the drug roulette, the easy fucking, the general mayhem and disorganization, the sleeplessness and emaciation was— miraculously—love. But where the Elders, in spite of the bankruptcy of their strategy, lingered hopelessly in some kind of piety and reverence before the unrealized ideal, these *teen-agers* sneered and yawned and lay about on couches watching old movies on television. What on earth could move them? Wars, revolutions and famine were, like *hang-ups* they didn't need, leftover downers from uncool generations, and please don't talk about peace and love and mystical unity, who're you kidding, a stone is a stone is a stone, a mind-blast, a way to get off for a while, where'd that stuff get you anyway, just a bunch of broken heads and prison cells and suicides, where's that at.

And Kathleen, dropping, chewing, snorting, smoking, flying into work hungover, and crashing after an all-night commune party, the dope paid for in her rent, an acid lab in the kitchen, and someone in the basement making false ID's, Kathleen, meanwhile, fell in love. Chris, the freak with the long blond hair who walked into a room so *cool* he might as well have been snapping his fingers, surrounded by freaky musicians, a token black and a bevy of girls, the crowd a whole lot cooler than any she had known before—she just had to have it. "Really, Chris was the worst person I've ever gone out with, the world was something he regarded with half-closed eyes, he was always stoned, nothing bothered or affected him, he had no feelings." Yet he was her first love, she guesses, but not so much for him as for his crowd, his style, the hint of decadence and a tragic end, people playing dangerously with imbalance and malnourishment, and not so much any of that as the desperation, at last, to get laid. Amazingly enough, she was still a virgin; to me, an unparalleled feat, how she had evaded her deflowering in that miasma of sensuality and self-enchantment, cock rock and careless groupies. How, in spite of the vulnerability when you're stoned and you can't say No, she said No. And now she was ready to lose this burdensome virginity, this condition no longer celebrated and rewarded among her friends, just another hang-up, what's so precious that you're hanging onto, uptight frigid broad, those other girls so *free*, they'd breeze into parties and go down for anybody, that's pretty liberated. Kathleen had been exempt because she was still a virgin, strange taboo, and now she wanted to be done with it. She settled on Chris as the lover worthy of the gift and dragged this half-asleep, stoned and sluggish boy into the bedroom, but he couldn't do it, couldn't get it up, his system so plugged by dope, and so a virgin she remained. Poor Kathleen. It was just as well. "With our crowd, making love was 'balling', there was no reaching out to other people, I mean, you were considered hung-up if you tried to hang onto someone."

A virgin still, Kathleen quit her job in March, 1971, and, leaving her savings behind, packed up with a girlfriend and left for California. By CNR coach to Vancouver (the quintessential Canadian trip) and then hitch-hiking to San Francisco. She was a little late. If it was an odyssey to the capital of Peace/Love/Flowers she was undertaking, she was four years too late. It had blown away over the sea like ashes from a cremation. And the blackened, skeletal remains harbouring junkies, bikers, dealers, speed freaks, and petty thieves depressed and soured her. Nobody was singing in the streets any more or shaking camel bells at her as she walked by, there was no more free food in the Panhandle, no more Be-ins in the Park, no incense, mint tea, and gentle weed, no more in fact, of dabblings in Femininity; the whole territory from Haight-Ashbury to Hollywood had reverted to one vast preserve of macho. Assault and rape, vicious police, knife fights, and riots, worship of the needle and ram-headed gods, and the aggressive reunion of Vietnam veterans and Leftist heavies.

> In Berkeley I first realized that women in the Left were just used by men to fuck when they got tired of talking politics with each other. In the hostel, we would be sitting around playing cards and drinking coffee and the phone would ring; there's a party, any girls who want to fuck can come. The numbers of offers I got to pose for porno photos was incredible; I was given the line that they would help to raise money for the movement.

Up and down the coast she went, paranoid most of the time, eating only every second or third day, sleeping in sheds by the highway or abandoned apartments or in free churches and hostels, getting picked up by police who shoved her around at the station, yelling, why aren't you at home? And having a terrible time with men who enjoyed her defenceless-ness—"they'd ask where's your man? as if somebody should own me and when I said I didn't have one they'd swarm around me." Black men were the worst; they counted on her being too embarrassed to refuse them for fear of being labelled a racist. In their war with Whitey they treated white women as fair game, a stand-off between two studded cocks in the ring with a female body at the stake, winner take her.

> They'd come to us and ask if we had a place to crash and we'd say Yes. Then they'd accuse us of hating blacks, and at first I'd say, No, No, that's not true, but when it kept happening like that—they'd never leave us alone—I'd just say, Fuck off, you coons. I'd scream at them—especially after the one time I did accept an invitation, and almost got raped by two guys at the house.

It was, she says, her period of being the strongest feminist.

And then, finally, Kathleen was deflowered, as they used to say in a more paternalistic and protective time. In California she was so close to being raped at any second that the fear of being a virgin when it happened drove her down to the beach one night with a man she'd met on the road, and there, where there would be no trace of blood left behind, she got drunk and he got drunk and he never noticed her virginity. He fell asleep right away, and she says she was pleased that he did not have the satisfaction of the masculine boast, *I* made her a woman. As for birth control, she never gave it a thought. Neither, for that matter, did he.

> For a year now I've voluntarily withdrawn from the sexual race, and it doesn't upset or frustrate me in the least. I may be willing now to go "shopping", maybe pick up guys if they interest me. I like unpretentious men with no male ego. Perhaps I don't miss sex because I haven't particularly enjoyed it in the past, and have had few orgasms. And anyway, sex really does interfere with what I'm doing; I've got to study on Saturday nights.

Sometimes she thinks she should have waited until she had found someone she really cared about, maybe even loved, before she gave up on virginity. At least you could avoid—if the first sex act really is full of psychic consequences—the fatal imprinting of hostility, fear and regret, and, if there is another way of making love, Kathleen hasn't found it.

> Most of my sex life, when I consider it, has been lousy, because I don't like to be dominated, and that's what happens in sex. The men I've slept with have always wanted to dominate. At the least sign of sexual aggression from me they couldn't get off. I haven't yet resolved how to make love without being concerned about the power plays in which I'm supposed to lose.

It is an observation that never occurred to me until, married and relatively domesticated, I ploughed into feminist texts. Sure sex had often been lousy, but I had not thought I could do something about that, I had not considered, as Kathleen has, that I could withdraw my body from such dismal use and refuse any compromise with sexual imperialism. But even that can only be a tactical retreat—we do, after all, want to be able to love men as well as each other—and if my generation was still involved in submission, Kathleen is only committed to sedition.

Had the eighteen-year olds learned anything, had they watched us threshing about between the loveless sheets, yelping sentimental endearments to drown out the sounds of hatred and revenge, and had they drawn conclusions? Yes, but only the obvious ones and not, for instance, the refusal to use the body as a weapon in an elemental battle of wills. "When I look back on my love life, right up to now, it's been pretty cynical, it's been power plays all the way, Me Tarzan, You Jane, take that and that!" The conclusion they drew, I guess, was that balling was balling and you'd better play it straight, up front, and drop the phoney emotional crap, be cool that is. Sex, said the boys, was balling, fucking, screwing, banging, and the girls, opening their legs said, okay, any way you want it.

And, then, when you are no longer a virgin, how do you say No? Your fear of the unknown had been your only defence, what can you summon up from your nightmares to protect you now? A new fear worked against the old, the terror that, if you never said Yes, you'd never get love either. Or maybe a new casualness, sex is no big thing, why not spare myself a hassle, maybe then he'll leave me alone. Kathleen hitched back to Toronto, without money, stopping off along the way in taverns. She'd wait long enough (never very long) and get free beer and food, chatting up the men, a French-Canadian, an Elvis Presley fan, a deaf-mute who handed her his motel key along with his begging card. "It happened a lot, I got drunk and went home with whoever I'd been drinking with. It didn't bother me that much at the time because I couldn't remember a thing in the morning." She spent time standing on the side of the Trans-Canada Highway between Medicine Hat and

Regina, content to stay for hours contemplating the prairie (she'd read the short stories of Laurence, Roy, and Ross), and along the way would listen to the tales of women who'd spent a lot of time on the road. They were mostly tales about sexual attacks: "there was Pat who had been sexually used and abused since age fourteen and who was very beautiful but who thought she was ugly, ugly." And she swore, of course, *she* would never become like that, so screwed-up, pitiable, punished and gutless—"why the hell wouldn't they ever fight back?" Kathleen, you can tell by now, is a survivor.

Back in Toronto, she applied for admission to grade thirteen in a middle-class collegiate, got a part-time job as a supermarket cashier, found a little flat on Queen Street East and went on welfare. The experience was decisive: she now plans to become a legal-aid lawyer, working for the poor, that is, working for women. When her first landlord discovered that she was on welfare, he removed the door to her flat. The superintendent, objecting to her having friends in, told her he wasn't running a brothel. She subsisted on beans, macaroni, and rice.

She sat for hours in welfare waiting rooms, "the most depressing places in the world", sharing the space with haggard women, screaming children and dying winos, reading all the signs that said Don't! and noticing that the offices of the bureaucrats had carpets, paintings and fine furniture, "as if they were drawing a line between themselves and the poor people. Clerks and social workers definitely give you the feeling you're doing something bad, but I didn't have much trouble with them that way; I told them my father doesn't believe in educating females, that he'd thrown me out of the house and that I was a genius in search of an education." No doubt the clerks' co-operativeness was based on the assurance that she was upwardly mobile, potentially a good bourgeoise.

> Once a month you can expect your cheque not to arrive and then you're given the runaround from office to office, a deliberate hassle to keep you in your place. Going to

banks was an experience, too, tellers throwing the money in your face, Why don't you get a job? or yelling, All welfare recipients stand in this line! making you feel like something that crawled out from under a rock; some banks wouldn't cash my cheques at all. I asked the guy, Listen, do you think the Government of Canada is going to rip you off?

She hit a low of self-respect, their message getting through, You bum! Drinking and going back with men to their apartments and then running out at the last minute, putting on her clothes and saying, Fuck off, fuck off, leave me alone. It was her last bout with ambivalence, the last time she believed anybody telling her she was a lower form of life. After that she went clear.

Answer to "If I Were a Carpenter"

Yes, we've decided that tomorrow is our own.
Yes, we realize that we'll often be alone.
I'll not offer up my life.
On the altar of some man
He must love me for what I am.
Not just a part in his plan.

I'll not hide myself beneath a feminine face
I'll not cook or bake or bear or keep my place
I'll not sell my soul for paradise
Like some piece of merchandise
My future for all his love is an unjust price.
(Kathleen, 1969)

Kathleen began with the idea that she would get what she wanted, progressed to the observation that her sex was inconveniencing her, developed the awareness that this was a problem for all women and ended (in her story so far) with an apocalyptic vision of a future world dominated by the female super-race.

Even the feminist Shulamith Firestone isn't radical enough for me. She says that the perfect society would be classless, sexless and cultureless. My feeling is that men and women aren't equal at all. Women are superior. But for the present I accept the egalitarian ideal because that's the route feminism will have to take initially. The reason I think women are superior to men is that even as an oppressed group they have been 'great' people and some have even been great in the masculine sense. Imagine what women will be able to be when the shackles are off!

In this, as in other ways, she advances beyond me. It is not, by any means, that I would not follow her there, it is that I cannot; too much of me is invested in keeping the peace with the patriarchs, soothing, reassuring, and enlightening them, measuring "up" to them, bedazzling and beguiling them, while at the same time still trying to live with them in harmony and equity instead of in fear and disgust. That's about as far as I can go.

But Kathleen goes farther. She is more integrated than I am, more coordinated in her feminism and her emotions and infinitely surer of getting to where she wants to go. Where I, working as a journalist, am as much involved in the need to outwit Norman Mailer as in the desire to speak to sisters, Kathleen is going to be a feminist lawyer, working only for and with women, and is ambitious to do something conclusive about rape, prostitution, and marriage laws; where I still stand, groaning, in front of a mirror, comparing myself unfavourably as much with Yoko Ono as with Faye Dunaway, Kathleen doesn't give a damn and is studying karate: "I decided at the beginning of the university year that I had time for one extra interest—a love affair or karate. I chose karate." Where I, approaching thirty, agonize over a childless old age, Kathleen says she doesn't have a maternal instinct and that is that. Nor does she sympathize with my fantasy of raising the perfect, non-sexist child: "If I raised a gentle, sensitive boy, he'd grow up to accuse me of emasculating him. As for daughters, I can reach more women's lives through my work than through one girl." Where I am still willing to be placatory and charitable when in the company of male chauvinists and to concede that some men are more progressive than others, Kathleen thinks that, as a group, men are contemptible. Where I am straddled, one foot firmly among the feminists, the other rooted in the circles of heterosexuality, marriage and the friendship of men, Kathleen looks forward to a love relationship with a woman and already calls herself bisexual, meaning, she says, how can she choose one sex over the other for warmth, affection, trust and orgasm? She also means that if, given our girlhood instruction and womanly occupations, women are the human beings who best know how to love, support and care for people, then we should live with each other, nourishing each other with our gifts and talents, instead of expending them on the one-way street of heterosexuality (women need nurturing too!); she means, too, that if you have been unhappy with men, maybe life will be kinder with women.

Where I, corrupted by doubt, ambivalence, and diffidence, cannot see where we women have advanced meaningfully over our great-grandmothers—we merely fight their fight with a new vocabulary—Kathleen is convinced that we will be able to look back on these years as our Dark Ages, that nothing on earth will be able to stop the advance of feminism, that women are, in fact, evolving as "the most intelligent and humane of the species". And above all, where my experience of being twenty and scared and assailable and full of false bravado has left me with a spiritual limp—I can see my whole generation walking down the road, dragging their stiff right leg behind them—so that I both long for a man's approval and yet disdain it, Kathleen laughs and laughs, delighted to live well enough without him.

This isn't the end of the story. Kathleen walks in ambiguities. Her life proceeds every which way in its potentials and the most she can do with it is show us what female liberation can look like in an unliberated society. And, as long as that is true, then Kathleen's styles and solutions are only stop-gaps for a bourgeois age. Perhaps her tenacity and solitude, egoism and self-sufficiency, satisfaction and good humour are only the other face of a coin we don't want to trade in at all. The resolution of that dilemma will be the end of us, as we know ourselves to be.

Living the Free-Lance Life: A Portrait of Abby Hoffman

BY VALERIE MINER

"All Star Defenceman Turns Out To Be Girl." blared the large banner headline on the *Toronto Telegram*. The kid with the boy's haircut and the boy's dash on the ice had fooled them, the paper's March 8, 1956 edition continued in amazement. Eight-year-old Abigail Hoffman had made it halfway through the season before they realized she was a girl. What was worse, by the time her secret was discovered, she had been invited to compete on the all-star team in Maple Leaf Gardens, and it was too embarrassing to kick her out. In the marshmallow world of the mid-fifties, Abby proved a cause célèbre for papers from the *Grand Forks South Dakota Herald*, to the *New York Times*, to the *Montreal Gazette*. By the next year, when the media had moved onto Sputnik and there was no room for cute masquerades, the Tee Pees dropped their hard-hitting defencewoman.

The newsphotos of the spunky little girl with the brushcut and the baggy Tee Pee uniform are yellowing now—replaced with half-tones of a strong, slender, intricately well-modelled woman moving down a track with force and grace. The leg muscles are taut; the arms move back and forth like gears in a Swiss watch. The brown Brillo hair is blown back by the wind, the grey eyes stare straight ahead, oblivious to the stands behind her which are filled with a popcorn blur of people. The twenty-seven-year-old woman is pushing, pulling, running—lithe, strong, determined, and alone.

This recent photograph is Abby's self-image—the athlete detached, developing, racing for the sheer satisfaction of effort.

65

Today she is one of Canada's hopes for the 1976 Olympics although she is nearing the end of her athletic career. She placed seventh in the 800 metre races at Mexico City and eighth at Munich. She garnered gold medals at the Pan American Games and the Commonwealth Games. She has served on more international track and field competitions than any other living Canadian.

Although Abby and I are the same age, she seems much more free—from the judgments of tradition and the claims of the future. I wonder if she is the certified "liberated woman"—the kind of individual my imaginary daughter might become. It seems too late for me and for most other women of my generation who were socialized into the "woman's role". But Abby grew up without the feminine constraints about dress, behaviour, worth, and power. Her family encouraged her to set her own standards. When she was little, she was called "off-beat". Her mother was called "eccentric". The cliché today is "liberated". The cost has been reduced from the ostracism in the fifties to mere detachment in the seventies. Abby says she doesn't mind the isolation; she has always been an outsider.

Abby considers herself primarily an athlete, but she has also surfaced with an independent identity as a university teacher and a political activist. The eight-year-old non-conformist has grown up to be a vehement critic of commercial sport exploitation, of sedentary university society, and of colonialism in the Third World. She is, perhaps, a woman of our generation in her ambivalence about a single career. But she is almost unique in the degree of her success. She seems unburdened by the traditional anxieties about her strength and ability.

Abby lives outside the mystique of the female body. From a distance, she is an androgynous figure. She never wears dresses or make-up. She is unfamiliar with the prescribed feminine gestures and accoutrements. Her hand movements are precise, not delicate. She strides rather than walks. In fact when she goes into Eaton's, she is often greeted with "May I help you Sir?" "Oh, yeah, it happens all the time. I just take it as part of my absurdist view of the world."

Abby is proud of her body, liberated with it in a sense most of us could never imagine. She says, "I don't care if I fit the social stereotype. An athlete learns just how superficial those definitions are. You know what your body can do. You're aware of fitness and form." Although Abby would cringe at being called a "beautiful woman", she is a sensual person: vibrant complexion, fresh, bright smile, clear eyes, well-toned limbs. Her lithe movements remind me of a bird—not a delicate sit-in-her-nest type of bird—more of a searching, swooping bird of prey. Maybe an osprey. She is stimulated by physical challenge. Her very presence is a subtle admonition. She makes me all too aware of my futile attempts to hide or shed the extra seven pounds of flab. I mean, there she is—someone who is in tune with her body, someone who doesn't feel weighed down by the classic dichotomy between a woman's sexuality and her intellect. Abby says, "I can't relate to not relating to my body. I don't know why I'm different from other women. I guess it's my general orientation to the world—'Screw you.'"

She grew up in that weird corner house on Glendonwynne Road in Toronto where you could look right through the drapeless windows. The neighbourhood kids always wondered why there was no TV in the living room. Queerest of all: there was no living room, just a large, empty, terrazzo tiled area with cupboards along the wall chock-full of sports equipment—an indoor hockey rink. When property tax officials tried to assess her for running a school, Abby's mother explained that she wasn't running an institution, just a home, thank you. Nobody seemed to understand why the idosyncratic Hoffmans drove around in a blue panel truck when everybody else was flashing two-tone sedans with V-8 engines and fancy tail-fins. They couldn't appreciate why the Hoffmans spent evenings together in the workroom, painting, and modelling, and reading, rather than watching *Perry Mason* and *Gunsmoke*, or why they took rock hunting hikes in the summer instead of driving down to Miami's air-conditioned, cut-rate motels. The closer they came to this household, the more eccentric it seemed. Sam Hoffman shared the shopping and cooking and cleaning. He washed his own clothes by hand. They didn't have a washing machine or an electric mixer or a vacuum cleaner or . . . because they spent their money on books and a country cabin. There wasn't much money, anyway, from Sam's salary as a paint company chemist and Dorothy's income as a nursery school teacher, especially since Dorothy paid the housekeeper a little bit more than she earned herself. The neighbours couldn't understand that at all....

Dorothy shaped Abby's independence. Dorothy Medhurst, swimmer and basketball star, the artist who dropped out of Central Technical School to work at the Art Gallery of Ontario with Arthur Lismer and later became a teacher without any professional training. The handsome blonde woman who wore rimless glasses and straight wool suits in the petticoated fifties has always retained her maiden name. She didn't see anything peculiar in having a job. She came from a long tradition of working women. Her grandmother had always worked as a tailor's assistant. How else could she survive after she shed her worthless husband? And Dorothy's mother established herself as a bookkeeper after she, in turn, left Mr. Medhurst. Dorothy grew up in twenty different rooming houses in Toronto's Cabbagetown. Dorothy always felt lucky to spend so much time with her mother—much more than the kids with two parents—reading and talking and going to movies. And her mother genuinely valued her freedom. She said that she paddled her own boat and that the sinking or swimming was up to her. Her Scots Presbyterian independence supported most of the unpopular causes of the day. She read Simone de Beauvoir, Eleanor Roosevelt, Agnes McPhail. She passed on her own temperate feminism to her daughter and grand-daughter.

The Hoffmans were a close, but not affectionate family. "We never spent a lot of time hugging and kissing," declares Abby with traces of little girl distaste in her voice. Paul, Muni, Abby, and Benny were all encouraged to compete in organized sport. It drew the four diverse personalities together—Paul, who wanted to grow up and become a solitary geologist; Muni, the sociable kid with all the girlfriends who wanted to be a garbageman with five children; Abby, the indomitable sprite, who looked forward to making a fortune as a gold prospector; and Benny who declared that he would like to become a cloud. The family's self-sufficiency lessened the need for outside social life. Throughout school Abby was always on the periphery. "We were taught that the other circles weren't important, that you had to have your own circle, your own set of principles." So began Abby's race against her own standards of perfection.

As we sit in her downtown Toronto apartment, Abby shows me another newsphoto from her large, blue scrapbook—a grinning four-year-old girl treading water in the Humberside Collegiate pool. Sports constitute her earliest memories and she says she will always define herself as an athlete. "It's very hard to explain; there's just something in my personality that draws me to sport." The stimulation and determination and discipline have clearly shaped her self-image. On the table next to us are piles of Xeroxed papers for her socio-economic study of Canadian women's sport. Scattered on the make-shift couch are several articles about political exploitation of sport in South Africa, the topic of her Ph.D. thesis. She hands me a copy of "Super-Jock in Decline: Liberating Sport from Sexist Stereotypes", which she has written for *Canadian Dimension*. Four gold medals are hung casually on the doorknob.

Abby played most of her early hockey on the terrazzo front room floor or at the artificial rink across the street. She would race home for lunch, slurp down her soup with the skates still around her neck, and run back to the ice. Her energetic family encouraged her hiking, swimming, hockey, running. Abby always wore trousers, partly because of these activities and partly because of Dorothy's pragmatism. Why shouldn't girls wear slacks? Their legs get cold in the winter, too. Besides, there were so many perfectly good corduroys in the house. The only dress Abby would wear was her Brownie uniform, much to the indignation of her teachers. And on several vacations, she and her mother were evicted from campground washrooms because they were mistaken for men in their short hair and pants. Abby recalls, "That hurt, because when you are six, you're insecure enough about reaching the door handle without someone telling you that you should be in the men's room."

Abby didn't have many girlfriends. "Girls are dumb in the head," the star Tee Pee defencewoman told the newspaper interviewers. No doubt the idea originated with her brothers, but she developed her own disdain for girls' docility. "They got in the way of the hockey puck and they cried when you threw snowballs at them." The first girlfriend she remembers is someone she tied up with skipping rope. She was alienated from girls because of their lack of skill as much as because of her lack of enthusiasm for Jr. Pillsbury Cookbooks and Betsy dolls. In school, she was separated from most of the other kids because of her sports prowess. She began competitive swimming when she was six. In junior high, she was distracted from the traditional pre-teen anxieties and activities by preparing for the Ontario Swimming Championships.

Abby never considered herself a female jock—just someone with a different interest. Once before a high school race, a woman approached her and warned that track would hamper her chances of having children. She told the woman to go to hell.

If the other kids thought that the Girls' Athletic Association was weird, she made equally devastating judgments about the inanity of their party scene. While most of her peers were struggling with the latest dance steps or the new cheerleader routines, Abby was testing *her* coordination for the Tokyo Olympics.

What you feel at the beginning of a race is a great deal of strength, a great deal of speed, a great deal of power and dynamism. The fear you had—the apprehension—is dissolved when the gun is fired. Now almost each tenth of a second is an exercise in total concentration. It's a question of internal harmony. You program yourself to hear your coach's signal, the cadence and breathing of the other runners. Similarly you focus your eyes like a camera lens—ten feet ahead—and you don't take in anything else. You're consistently aware of your position. You have to know who's in front of you and who's behind. Who's moving. Who can't handle the group. Who appears to be running smoothly. You're also aware of how you feel physically. Most of the fear is gone. But if someone does something unexpected—someone is running faster than you anticipated—you say, 'Christ, I can't keep up. That has ruined my tactical plan to run the race.' Or you may begin to wear out before the end of the race, at the final kick. You may reach the lactic acid saturation point.

The first sensation at the end is relief. If the race has gone well, with a great deal of concentration, you should feel like it has taken two hours instead of two minutes. The change you've put your body through is fantastic— from the point of being able to do anything to the point of being physically incapacitated. After a race, you just stand and put your hands on your knees for a few seconds, until some of the lactic acid has cleared out of your body. You warm down for a few minutes to get yourself back on the regenerative cycle. If you have done well, you are exhilarated. Regardless, you have a tremendous feeling of relaxation. You have no inhibitions of letting your body act of its own accord. You can't imagine feeling any more lack of control, any more intense release.

Abby was shaping her own priorities when most of us were still scrutinizing *Mademoiselle*'s "Twelve-Hints-To-Attract-A-Neat-Date" articles. Today she doesn't seem the least bit nostalgic for her missing Shelly Fabares youth. She dated a few times, had a couple of friends, but she wasn't one of the bevies of Canadian girls who spent their afternoons in front of the TV gossiping and guzzling Coke. Athletics provided her with too many alternatives—travelling, newspaper coverage, physical stimulation. "Sure there were days when I said, 'Shit, I wish I was a cheerleader . . . ' or 'I wish I had *her* looks,' but there weren't many." There was enough satisfaction in sports and in that perennial intervening variable, her family.

She said it never bothered her, the way it worried the rest of us academic wallflowers, that she didn't get invited to the Junior Prom or the Senior Ball. She would have had a harder time explaining to Dorothy how she got talked into the bourgeois affair than she had facing her own romantic rejection. She wasn't one of us who spent hours before the mirror, struggling to get the eyeliner straight, mixing white with pink lipstick for just the right frosted shade or blushing on Revlon's natural tone. She just washed her face in the morning before she went to school. What would she say to Dorothy if she came home with a little plastic make-up kit?

She didn't spend hours in Eaton's agonizing over the neatest colour of Shetland mix-and-match sweater to go with her Capezio shoes. She did face one crisis, however, the catastrophe of frizzy hair. What do you do with a Brillo pad when the other girls have such straight, sleek manes? She even went to the local drug store to inquire about a hair-straightening kit, but she couldn't figure out how to use it. Besides, how could she explain it to Dorothy? "I would have been laughed right out of the house if I had done any of those soppy teenage things," Abby says, laughing now, herself. So Abby was too busy, too perceptive, too isolated for the adolescent anxieties which confined most of our generation.

In university she continued training for the Mexico City Olympics. People questioned her combination of athletics and academics more than her status as a woman athlete. Her University of Toronto friends couldn't understand why she ran, and track friends couldn't relate to her studies. But their lack of empathy never bothered her. "Most people don't talk to me at all about my sports. They don't say, 'It's weird that you do all this running my dear.' That may be a sign of being odd in itself. I mean, who knows how to carry on a conversation with a female runner? Christ, there aren't too many of us around." The only confrontation between the individualist athlete and the traditional university occurred at the Hart House track during Abby's first year. She knew it was reserved for men, but she thought she'd try it, anyway. When she was thrown out, she didn't complain—she had survived the Tee Pees and there was no moral support from a women's movement then—she just found another place to train. The discipline and routine of studying added to the discipline and routine of sports, distancing her further from other people.

"I guess I use the isolation of sports as an excuse to stay apart," she tells me one day. This is an unusually introspective response from Abby. Ironically, the closer I come to her, the more distant I feel. I am at ease in her social ambience—the academic subsistence level life-style. Her old flat reminds me of my own, ten blocks away in the same immigrant neighbourhood: the clinking debilitated radiator, the cheap furniture, the stacks of books and records, the same magazines lying open on the floor. As we sit on her cheap kitchen chairs, I realize that as much as I identify with her domestic surroundings and political reference points, I am very detached from her. Her independence is sustained by a concentration on work. She does not diffuse her energies into personal relationships.

She enjoys running for the sense of harmony with other women as much as for the competition. "One of the reasons I like being in a high level contest is the feeling of group rhythm. It becomes difficult to distinguish yourself from the other members of the race. When I was in the Munich Olympics, the difference between the first person and the last person in the final was 1.7 seconds. Obviously we went around the track with a great deal of harmony. You feel like all the runners are tied together on a string. It's a psychological and physical relationship. You could be very far behind, but if you're accelerating and decelerating with that lead person, you feel like you can reel her in. You're always aware of trying to beat the others. But everyone wants to put in a good performance together. It's a paradox: the group concept heightens the competition. I finished last at Munich, but I felt a great sense of satisfaction at the end because I had run my best personal time and because the race had been of such high calibre. I don't think I would have felt much more exhilarated if I had won."

As Abby approaches the end of her competitive years, she considers an advisory career in sport. Her current absorbtion is a book about the history of women in Canadian sport. She will discuss, for instance, the 1920s and '30s when the media coverage of women's athletics was similar to the press attention now focused on men's organized sport. There were regular women sports columnists. The softball games at Toronto's Kew Beach were broadcast on the radio. Many of the participants were working-class women in their twenties. The popularity petered out in the mid-thirties as part of the conservative backlash of the depression, when women were persuaded to leave their jobs. Then the newspapers were crammed with reactionary articles declaring that sport wasn't healthy for women. "We're still recovering from the stereotypes," declares Abby. "We associate sport with men, with masculinity and masculine qualities. We have to break that down."

Abby becomes more and more animated as we move from her personal relationships to her social criticism. She leans the wooden chair against the counter of the persimmon and plum kitchen cupboards, pacing her quick comments out with her thin hand. Perhaps this is her most natural milieu—this world of socio-political hypothesis. As we drink tea from rough, handmade mugs, I wonder what Abby Hoffman is doing with the mundane sink-side accessories of Power Plus and Javex. Indeed, from *any* point of view her private life—the clutter of the kitchen sink or the raw edge of her emotions—seems spare in comparison to her public image.

Her most vociferous complaint about athletics focuses on a problem shared by men and women: commercial exploitation. She says professional athletics uses the talents of a few players and the interests of thousands of spectators for the corporate profit. She complains that the distinction between participant and observer just encourages "sloth", one of her favourite pejoratives "sloth" and "indolence".

At first I was disturbed by her kinetic personality. Obsessive compulsive? No, that's a fatuous, even jealous, observation. More probably she just inherited a healthy respect for effort from her active family. In fact, her whole energy is stimulated by and calculated for achievement. "People only use about half their body IQ," she admonishes with almost evangelistic fervour. "You can't accomplish anything if you sit around all day. In fact I think my mental capacity is only about three hours a day. If I don't get some exercise, I'm no good at academic work."

Assistant Professor Abby Hoffman teaches in the concrete, characterless Arts edifice which looks down over smaller, graceful buildings at Guelph University in Southern Ontario. This traditional Aggie campus, defined by flush-faced farm kids and housewives in homecoming buttons, seems an ironic contrast to Abby's radical urban sensibilities. But she likes the openness of these students. She sits confidently at the front of the room—behind one of the large white tables joined in a square. Her students don't call her "Professor Hoffman", nor do they call her "Abby". Somewhere in between, she holds their unclassified respect. Abby is scholarly but not esoteric, demanding, but not authoritarian. As she lectures, she draws in her breath, setting a hard edge to her voice. Her directness is a kind of reserve in itself. It inhibits people, establishing a protective distance.

Today in her seminar on Africa she is discussing "a typical example of the hysterical over-simplified coverage you get in *Time*", an article predicting the decline of apartheid in South Africa. She easily draws out her students' opinions, closely leading, but not impeding the discussion. When one fellow asks, "Aren't they offering the blacks more jobs to increase their buying power?" she answers excitedly, "OK, OK, but what are they giving the blacks really?" "Nothing, I guess." She continually refers them back to the other readings— encouraging one student to answer another. The spirited discussion closes with characteristic cynicism. "See, you have a great deal of fun when you read *Time* slowly."

We walk up to her office in this corporate academic building with its sleek elevators and carpeted hallways. Abby looks more like a frenetic student than a dignified scholar. She enjoys the classroom interaction as much as the academic preparation. She grins slyly as she admits the controversy she has created by teaching her classes on the Third World as studies in capitalist exploitation. Guelph is a conservative campus where professors tend to subscribe to the "All's right-with-the-world, colonialism-was-good-for-the-savages" theory. Obviously benign neglect was never one of Abby's philosophies. She prefers to teach part-time; she has no aspirations to professional prestige. She isn't dedicated enough to the institution of the university to care whether her students borrow essays. She just hopes to stimulate her classes sufficiently to do their own work. She prepares lectures diligently, leads class discussions enthusiastically, listens attentively to students' questions during office hours. But academia remains only one part of her free-lance life along with her running, her CBC work, and her political concerns.

The clutter of her small office illustrates the challenge of fitting together her jigsaw puzzle schedule. "Go to the book store at 3:00" is scrawled on an index card in the dial of the ringing phone. The small blackboard is cramped with scribbles, "See Bruce about study group". Piled on the floor are Xerox copies of an article, "Castro Has Evidence that U.S. Took Part in Coup", which are to be distributed in class. A map of the University of Guelph is falling off the back of the door. Her flip calendar is dated eleven days ago. Her jacket hangs on a wall peg—two felt pens sticking out of the pocket— convenient to grab when she dashes out the door.

Abby is the only female professor in her department. She says some of the women students relate particularly well to her, but she bristles at being called a card-carrying "role model". She has no qualms about women's ability. She declares vehemently that women are better organized and quicker witted than men—a reflection of her own self-image. The only discrimination she has encountered has been a reluctance to give her some of the department's busywork. But she doesn't want to climb Guelph's academic ladder, anyway. Perhaps the clearest indication of her immunity to academic chauvinism was her initial job interview. She wasn't asked any of the customary "female" questions about home and family. "There's something in my manner that's sufficiently intimidating that I don't get questions like that very often."

Her penchant for politics was stimulated, predictably enough, by the little Lenin library on Glendonwynne Road. Both parents were active in the Progressive Movement during the thirties; they were stomped by RCMP horses in Queen's Park in 1939. Just as Abby models her independence on her mother, she inherited her keen critical mind from her father. Sam Hoffman, who was once described in the *Toronto Telegram's* inimitable phrasing as "a retiring sort", exerted his influence around the household through passive resistance. He would proffer opinions about Continentalism and Stalinism and the ravings of Joe McCarthy—inconsequential platforms for domestic decisions, but formative stimuli to his children's analytical minds. Abby was taught to observe and interpret politics for herself.

At age five, she entered the University of Toronto School where she benefitted from the close student-teacher rapport. At Humberside Collegiate, where she was tracked into the "brain class", her favourite subject was history. She joined the model UN and became disillusioned with the liberal ideal of world government, "The kids at Upper Canada College always got to be the United States or Russia and the kids from schools like mine got to be Chad or Gabon. I'd say that's a pretty realistic lesson about world power. The rich wind up with all the territory." When she entered university, she wanted to study political science and become a diplomat or a civil servant. Like many of us who started college as liberals, studies radicalized her beyond the compromise required by government service. Instead, she opted for the detached role of political analyst.

Abby was never involved in the student movement at university she says, "because it was controlled by a small group of relatively incompetent men." Despite her parents' example, she has never participated in a demonstration—prime distinction between Abby's individualism and my idealism. At Berkeley I transferred the passionate righteousness of my conservative Catholic home to "the movement". We Catholics had an edge on revolution anyway, because of our pervasive guilt and our potent free wills. My emotional commitment to anti-war protest, the California Grape boycott, Third World autonomy—preceded my academic analysis. I wonder if I was not more representative of our generation. Abby's involvement was strictly intellectual. Sure, the "revolution" was ephemeral. But while I imagined myself in the vanguard, Abby was reading about the movement in the *Varsity*.

Today she infuses her ideology into her teaching, articles and speeches. Abby describes herself as "definitely more radical than NDP but she's alienated from the socialism that has splintered into the absurd, indistinguishable abbreviations of the New Left. "I guess you could call me an anarchist. I'm a nationalist, but I'm not naive enough to be fooled by the self-interest of some people's patriotism." She concedes, somewhat reluctantly, "I see a real benefit in making people believe in the perfectability of man. It makes life less hostile. But basically I believe that things are pretty screwed up and they're going to stay that way." Her politics, like her athletics and her academic career, are defined from the periphery.

Abby has to get back to Toronto to do a radio show the next morning, so she offers me a lift down the 401. Her old red Volvo bears no proclamations on the bumper. The only evidence of ownership is the eclectic mess inside—a shoebag and an electric kettle tossed on the back seat with *Only One Earth,* an ancient red sweater, and a yellowing *Globe and Mail.* Our conversation about politics has led to an argument about women's liberation.

Abby challenges the movement's political priorities. She says that capitalism—not sexism—should be the prime target in developing countries. She also complains that within Canada itself, sexism is just a middle class issue. "Society has got to change the role of women, but that's not the first thing you change. Sure, the basis of capitalism is the family and therefore the exploitation of women, but I can't place women at the beginning of my political analysis."

"But wait a minute," I interrupt, "Don't you realize that in any oppressed country, the most exploited people are the women? They have the lowest status and the least opportunity. They have to take orders from the men. They do all the shitwork."

I'm enjoying the sensation of having a spirited discussion rather than a detached interview with Abby. The relationship model and more of a . . . no, "sister" isn't the word, even I cringe at the sentimentality, more of a . . . contemporary.

"No, women *have* had a chance to contribute," she says. "Always. They've been in the background in the past. But that's changing now. . . . "

"Oh, really? How many women MP's . . . " It seems ironic to me as I look out the window, feeling our isolation from the other darkened cars and our own familiarity, that *we* should be arguing about feminism. The dispute belongs in the VW bug with the middle-aged man and his wife, or in the Buick stationwagon with the greying mother and the teenage daughter, or behind any one of the hundreds of other sets of whizzing headlights, but not in the old red Volvo with the two radical young women. Again, I feel the paradox of being near Abby. We are brought together by circumstance and life-style and ideology, but are still divided by her sober individualism and my passionate idealism, by her rational Presbyterian reserve and my romantic Catholic commitment.

"Yes, yes" she concedes. "I agree with that and I would think women have a lot to offer. I could see a lot of good coming from women's involvement in sports and politics."

It's another clash of style. She agrees with the end, but not with the means. Abby will never carry a picket sign outside the Department of Justice to demand Indian women's land rights or hand out leaflets at a beauty pageant. She has been tempted, she says, to accept an invitation to address a right-to-life rally and then to declare her support for abortion-on-demand. Although the suggestion is sardonic, her conviction about abortion is deep and personal. She had an abortion last year in New York State. Since then, she has been battling with the Ontario Medical Health Insurance Plan to give her coverage for it. "It's the principle of the thing—not the money—I'm doing it on my own, making phone calls, writing letters to officials. Maybe if I get coverage for it, some other women will too. But that's what the women's movement doesn't seem to understand—you can be doing something on your own. You don't have to wave around a placard."

She doesn't want to talk about the abortion, because, she says, it is just a personal matter. I try to convince her that unless more people speak out, the laws won't change. I explain that after I had an abortion, I found it helpful to share the experience with other women. She still refuses. The persistent journalistic fear that one is trespassing into private territory precludes further discussion.

Abby's distance from the movement is measured by the difference between most women's vulnerability and her own self-confidence. While she is increasingly aware of cultural and professional discrimination against herself and other women, she doesn't suffer much sexism in her personal life. If liberation is the development of independent identity, she underwent the process during her pre-adolescent years. Predictably, she is disappointed in the progress of other women, and rejects the stereotype of females as victims, "I don't relate to myself as a person who has been discriminated against. My self-perception as a woman isn't the traditional one, and it's not the one seen by the women's movement either."

Her relationship with George, the man she lives with, is unconventional, even for a generation pretending to thrive on the other side of marital convention. She spends half her week at the cabin near Guelph and the other half at the Toronto apartment. They both come and go as they please. Abby enjoys their brief times together. She declares that she could never have a traditional marriage or live with anyone over a protracted period of time because she is too willful.

George and Abby share the household chores. "Cleaning is a joint activity; that means nobody does it." They wind up in some traditional roles by default. One afternoon George doesn't know what to do with the chicken wings, so Abby cooks dinner. Meanwhile, she can't figure out what's wrong with the Volvo, so he spends half an hour outside repairing it. They share all the decisions. She explains, "At first I thought it would be good for the man to decide things, I guess because it always was the opposite when I was growing up. I let it go like that until he made a few wrong decisions. Now we're fairly egalitarian. I mean, much more so than in most households where the decision-making goes according to the economic contribution. I bring in most of the money here and I don't treat George like a wife."

Their relationship started with an intellectual attraction and their domestic atmosphere is one of ideological and temperamental confrontation, "I have the feeling that if I were around any more we wouldn't get along. Sometimes we ask each other, 'Don't you want to go on a trip or something?' We never gave it much thought when we moved in together. I mean we never thought it was forever or that it would restrict either of us. George socializes separately. I don't, but I go where I want and when I want. I stick with the guy because I really like him. We enjoy a lot of things together. We both have a sense of the absurd. We like to laugh at how fucked up the world is."

Abby has had several relationships with men but wouldn't consider lesbianism an extension of her body's liberation. "Goodie for the radical feminists, but I'm not interested in a homosexual relationship. I could tell you that running around the track with other women was a sublimated sexual experience. But that would be the biggest bunch of bull I ever fed anybody. Many people think sports is a replacement for sex. Well, you get kind of a cartharsis from sports; it's a cleansing, stimulating thing. I don't want to carry the analogy too far, but I guess you could say there's a building up to a climax, a getting lost in it, a feeling of release. I wouldn't say that athletics is a replacement for sex. I do think that a certain kind of personality—a self-contained individual—is going to be more attracted to athletics. Someone who is very dependent on other people isn't going to go in for it."

Marriage promises little emotional reward to Abby. Convenience would be her only rationale for succumbing to a contract. "Maybe if the man I was living with was rich and it would make things easier legally. . . . " Abby is ambivalent about motherhood. She would like to be a parent in about ten years, but worries she will be too old then to bear healthy children. And kids do bring hassles: the expense, the life-long commitment, the chores. On the other hand, she would enjoy the experience of watching someone develop and grow, of having someone around when she was older. She wouldn't care if she had sons or daughters.

Abby still sees her own parents at least twice a week. Her mother is her only close friend besides George. "Dorothy is energetic, entertaining, one of the most interesting people I know. She can talk about anything from the snakes of North-eastern Ontario to the Bauhaus. She's almost sixty and she goes on a three-week canoe trip every summer. She puts effort into everything she does. Next to her, I'm an indolent, slothful person."

The admiration is mutual. Dorothy respects Abby's humour and drive and athletic prowess. Dorothy gave me an interesting perspective into Abby's future, since the daughter is almost the mirror image of the mother's youth. All the edges have softened with Dorothy. Her bright blue eyes are cushioned with smile creases. Her lean body is kitten-limber as she sits on a first grade stool, her head on her hand, the elbow resting on her raised knee. Dorothy still wears the rimless glasses. The bright purple and pink smock shows that the Scots Presbyterian bookkeeper's daughter has brightened and relaxed over the years. Through Dorothy, I can see Abby's sometimes abrasive arrogance developing into a graceful individualism. Abby, who was made in her mother's image, admits that her parents' expectations are the only ones which still affect her. I feel more comfortable with Abby, seeing her reflection soften with the years. If she keeps stride with Dorothy, she will finish alone, perhaps, but not so isolated.

Meanwhile, aside from George and her mother, Abby has three or four other friends whom she sees during the course of her working day or if they happen to trip through her apartment. She doesn't go to parties or make luncheon dates or visit other people's homes. "I find friends a real burden, actually. I don't get a great deal of pleasure discussing my affairs with other people. Everybody is going through exactly the same shit. I don't want to impose my troubles on other people and I don't want them to bum me out with their problems.

"People think that if you're not particularly gregarious, you're some kind of misanthrope. It seems necessary to justify the pleasure of one's own company. There is a lot I like to do on my own. The athletics. The reading. And I find it much easier to deal with the world alone. There are some practical explanations, too. I've always been doing something different from most of my contemporaries. My family got me used to a non-existent social life. It's not a question of making an overt choice to be detached. I'm not really conscious of what the alternatives are."

So Abby spends most of her time alone—long morning drives to the university, afternoons jogging in the park, evenings studying and correcting papers. She goes to films by herself; walks around for hours in the solitude of the Toronto Islands. She spends her life trying to meet her own standards.

We are approaching the Toronto exit and the end of our last talk. I wonder if I, Valerie Miner, the free-lance journalist, know Abby Hoffman, the free-lance person. I see her striving for the intellectual satisfaction in her politics, for the physical satisfaction in her athletics. These goals are her raison d'être. She gauges herself by the running rather than by the winning. Effort is her strongest moral imperative. She explains. "Athletes have to set high expectations to reach high levels. Even though most of the time these expectations are absurd, you realize that in the past it was possible for you to do this completely unrealistic thing, so you have to keep trying." She says I'll never understand her unless I can sympathize with the runner who trained for ten years to improve her record by a tenth of a second. I mention the obsession to write one simple, perfect sentence. She accepts the analogy. She says that she doubts whether anyone could express her character on paper when she can't even analyse it herself. If her arrogance is the victory of time over space, mine is the synthesis of perceptions and words. She nods and says I have come as close to her identity as possible.

I ask her why she let me get so close. "That's a good question," she laughs. "Ego and curiosity maybe. I say, 'Ah, the fuckin' interviewer's coming.' But I do care what other people think about me. I guess I'm not nearly as good at telling people to get lost as I fancy myself. And there's the social thing. My social interactions are quite structured. This started out as an interviewer-subject thing, but it could develop into kind of an accidental friendship. To the extent that I like communicating with other people, I like structured situations. Being interviewed is OK." I've never been called a "fuckin' interviewer" before, but I don't mind it from Abby. It implies a certain intimacy in her absurdist coterie. I would like to think she's right about an accidental friendship, that, some day, I'll be one of those people tripping through her apartment. But right now I can't think of any more structured situations for us.

I wonder about that imaginary daughter of mine. I would like her to be as "liberated" as Abby. I would like her to play hockey and argue politics. It's too late for me to act so freely with my body, to feel so uninhibited about my appearance, to be unrestrained enough to say "Screw You" as much as I would like. Abby's sense of freedom is a model for my someday child. However, I hope she will share some of my empathy and gentleness. I want her to realize, as I eventually did, that Abby is an individual as well as a prototype. She can emulate Abby without copying her. Hopefully, then, I won't find it so hard to be close to my daughter.

When I think about Abby now, I don't focus on any of the

times we had together, the visits to each other's flats, or the telephone conversations, or the twelve reels of tape. I don't dwell on the photos in the blue scrapbook, the Tee Pee hockey player, or the high school swimmer, or the adult Olympic runner. I think of her in the future—ten years from now—running around High Park; lithe, strong, determined, and alone.

The Education of
Madeleine Parent

BY ERNA PARIS

For 35 years, Madeleine Parent has lived in a hornet's nest—
quite by choice. Her reputation as a union organizer is formidable, and whenever her name is mentioned in labour circles,
emotion runs high. She's either loved or hated. There's no
moderation where Madeleine is concerned—which is not
surprising, because she really is an outrageously bold woman
and she has stepped on some very big toes. She has lived
through some of the worst periods of Canadian anti-labour
history; she has been the victim of direct persecution during
the Duplessis regime; she's been arrested more times than it's
worth counting; and she's been tried in Quebec for seditious
conspiracy—and convicted.

Madeleine's a woman of iron-willed conviction, and organizing unskilled workers has been the focus of her entire life—
more important than marriage, family, or friendship. She's a
"true believer", as Eric Hoffer put it, and her single-minded-
ness places her in a long, historic tradition of zealots whose
passion has led them along strange and difficult ways.
Madeleine became a force in our recent trade union history
because she learned early to stand alone and dig her heels in,
and because she had that peculiar chemistry of leadership that
can turn other people into "believers" and move them to
action.

Madeleine Parent is 56 this year. She survived Duplessis
nicely, and she prevails—by wile, by wit, by tactic—by pure
faith.

The colossus I've described is 5′ 2″ tall, a tiny woman with small bones and fine features, a neat orderly woman who wears a black cloth coat, purple cloth gloves, and a purple felt hat. She flicks invisible dust off a distinctly feminine pink skirt and sweater set and crosses her legs properly as she sips tea. She smiles a lot, warmly, and listens carefully when people speak to her. She's a woman whose ordinary conversation in both English and French is remarkably precise, for whom the right word, the perfect word is always available, whose speech rolls off her tongue in tightly-constructed sentences with commas, dashes, and emphatic underlining. That's the result of long training. One of the few teachers she respected as a child taught elocution, and since then she's had lots of soapbox experience learning what words and tone to use to evoke the desired response, just how to awaken the sense of thwarted justice and wounded dignity that lies below the surface in all of us, and how to kindle the right combination of hope and anger in the breast of a depressed factory worker. She's learned what words and tone to use in tough bargaining sessons with hostile management who would as soon drown her as listen to her, and how to deal with their shrewd lawyers. She's learned what words and tone are needed to enlist the aid of the press, a technique that was quite successful during her trial for seditious conspiracy when she managed to embarrass Duplessis publicly, and a technique that was still right up front as we struggled for control of our early sessions together, she naming the friends and many enemies of her career, I insisting that I was interested in her *response* to the events of her life, beyond the events themselves. . . .

I first saw Madeleine Parent in March 1974 at an International Women's Day celebration in Toronto. She was one of the speakers on the platform and she looked like somebody's kindly mother, or a schoolteacher, or perhaps a gentle aunt. She listened to the others attentively, kept her hands folded carefully in her lap, and smiled readily. But when she began to speak, the shuffling and whispering in the hall stopped. It wasn't just what she was saying, though her comments about the conditions of immigrant women factory workers in the textile trade were interesting enough. It was *the way* she spoke, each word emerging rounded and separate, like brightly-coloured beads on a string, polished, shiny, linked together, but clearly individual. Her voice rose at the end of every phrase and paused on an up note, keeping the listener hanging, and it never levelled off until she had finished telling us what she wanted us to know.

She insists that she is not introspective, that since she decided to become a union organizer when she was 20 years old and a student at McGill University, she has never looked back. There have been moments when she has questioned the way she has handled things, and there have been moments of fear for herself or for Kent Rowley, her husband and co-organizer from the beginning in the United Textile Workers of America (American Federation of Labor) and now in the Canadian Textile and Chemical Union, a member of the Canadian Confederation of Unions which they founded together in 1968. But she has never questioned the original decision, she says, through all the difficulties of 35 years.

And let us not underestimate what those difficulties have been. As a cherished enemy of Maurice Duplessis she was in constant danger, for Duplessis used the police to harass individuals he disliked. People were arrested and homes were ransacked under the "Padlock Law", which meant that police were able to search without a warrant. As the object of personal and political witch-hunts during the cold war, Madeleine and Rowley were persecuted for being communists, though she denies that they were. Whether they carried cards seems irrelevant today. They were militant socialists, at the far left of the trade union political spectrum, and that was not a pleasant place to be in Quebec during the 1940s and the early '50s. She has fought management, government, the police, the

Church in Quebec, and union bureaucrats for whom the focus of union-management relations was only economic betterment and not social reconstruction.

In fact, Madeleine has fought dragons everywhere, and I'd say she has loved every minute of it. The passion is just behind her eyes. They light up like naked bulbs when she describes the succession of campaigns, fights, and struggles of her career. It is in her fists that clench, unconsciously, on the neat, pink skirt as she talks of "war", and it's in the undeniable excitement of her voice as she relives, thrilled, the moment at Valleyfield, Quebec, in August 1946, when 6000 striking textile workers won the day and defeated the provincial police.

> Duplessis and the Church mounted the attack on the strikers. The Church had organized special masses with a special appeal to workers who wanted to go back to work, the understanding being that when enough workers showed up to pray on a morning they'd march to the plant headed by the priest. So they did that one morning and the company goons brought them into the plant. All over town word spread that there were scabs in the plant, and the picket line had been broken and needed support. The news travelled like a prairie fire. The milkman brought the news, the baker, the butcher, the grocer, the delivery boy, the women in their backyards, almost everybody had worked in the mill or had a son or daughter there, and they all went over. By 11 a.m. there were 6000 people at the plant gates, men, women, adolescents, everyone went to the plant gates, and they stood there and they stood. And as the crowd grew and waited, angry but very disciplined, the provincial police aimed machine guns at them . . . at one point the police fired a gas bomb, and within very little time everyone had a rock, they literally tore up the pavement, and at one command, "fire", it was given in English, 6000 rocks were thrown. The battle carried on until 5 or 6 p.m. and in the course of the

day, the provincial police took out a white handkerchief. It was one of the rare cases in history where the police were beaten. . . .

Parent's language is the language of war. Hers is a black and white world of good and evil, of bogey-men profiteers and good-fairy workers, of fights and struggles for justice, of company goons, betrayals, stabbings, agents provocateurs, battles, and crises. It's a world seemingly without grey shadows or nuance, a Darwinian tooth and claw struggle for power and control.

> Asking me about whether I condone violence is like asking do I condone bombing by the Vietnamese people against the American invaders, she said in an interview with a Toronto paper in 1972. I don't think they would do it gratuitously, but they do it in self-defence. I've been in a lot of strikes and I've personally never thrown a rock. But I've seen our people do it, and I've known our people to do it many times. And I've also known that when they've refrained from doing it in the face of provocation, they were just mercilessly smashed. It's suicide not to take some action.

In 1924 when she was six years old, Madeleine's parents sent her to a Montreal school run by an order of cloistered nuns. Her family was well off—her father was an accountant and general manager for Dionne's, a prestigious Quebec grocery chain—and young French-Canadian girls from that social background in Montreal were boarded in convent schools. That was the social convention, and the way the world turned. But Madeleine says it almost killed her. "To go behind the gates with the cloistered nuns was just like being put into the tombs and going back to the Middle Ages, like going to my death. Nobody seemed to belong to my era or that of my father or mother or aunts or uncles. I was terrified and I fought and I fought. That's where I learned to fight.

"I had nightmares in the dormitory and kept everyone awake and finally they had to take me home! I was ill for several months after.

"I stayed home until I was seven and in the autumn they sent me to another convent school. This time it was a day school and the nuns were not cloistered, but for the first year I didn't get over the earlier trauma. As soon as I arrived home at the end of a day and saw my mother I burst into tears. I was so relieved to be free—to belong at home and not to the nuns. When you're seven that's crucial. You don't have that many defences."

The trauma of the nuns was probably the most important experience of her entire life and the soil from which the particular shape of her future sprang. The memory of helplessness and powerlessness has clung to her always, to be summoned forth, smelled, and tasted at will with the intensity of original terror. She learned quickly to respond to others whom she sensed felt that way too, and would rage on their behalf. One of the little girls at school was poorer than the rest, and the nuns chastised her often and publicly because her bills weren't paid. Madeleine defended her and learned a little about hypocrisy at the same time. "I felt that it was horribly unjust without understanding too well. Here they were preaching charity and everything else, and the child was only seven or eight years old. I defended her and she became my best friend. I also became aware that I was her only friend."

Having learned about adults and clay feet it wasn't too hard to buck the system, and Madeleine soon became known as an independent little one who thought about what she said and did rather carefully. When the priest visited the class and asked how many little girls were planning to become nuns, she was the only one to decline the honour. "It seemed perfectly natural not to raise my hand, and the fact that everyone else did didn't matter at all. The nun asked me what I would do and I said 'I'll get married.' I didn't think of remaining single; if you remained single, you became a nun."

94   *The Education of Madeleine Parent*

When Madeleine was 12, she was sent to Villa Maria, a convent school where boarding was compulsory during the final two years. But she boarded for only one year before she quit in protest at the way the school was managed. This time she was older and better able to cope and "fight" as she continually puts it. "Fighting was an internal thing. I just didn't accept what they did and thought, and I became completely convinced that this was not the kind of life and system I wanted to live in.

> During the year I boarded I saw something I had guessed but never seen before, and that was the horrible treatment dealt out to the maids. Most were from the poor farming areas of Quebec, or else they were Acadians from New Brunswick. They were second class on the lowest level. The nuns kept about 80 per cent of their wages to mail to their parents, and gave them one or two dollars a month as spending money when they were allowed out.

By now, the politicizing process was already well under way and it came from that early, tearing experience of helplessness. She was also turning away from the Church, unable to understand why the social practices she observed were so different from the preachings she believed. She had had a "church education", dogma and religious instruction were as close and familiar as conversation and three meals a day, and at age 15 she was neither intellectually nor emotionally prepared to empty her life of its content. What would fill the void? But she did take a step to the left with the Dominicans, who were challenging the elitist and more orthodox Jesuits. The Dominicans were taking up social causes such as the education of poor children, and that was enough for the time being. It wasn't until she became a student at a Montreal upper class private school called Trafalgar that she seriously questioned her religious beliefs.

From school to school, stage to stage, the straight and narrow (even puritanical) line of her development extended, and the specific focus of her personality became clearer. Each successive observation, each event, though it might have gone unnoticed by another child, became part of a continuum of growing awareness, like tiny electrical shocks of recognition. At Trafalgar, Madeleine began to shape these impressions into ideas and to present them with sharp-edged clarity. She had to—Trafalgar was an English-language school, and the Protestant beliefs and background clashed sharply with her own. "I fought with myself trying to keep an identity of my own. They believed the Blessed Virgin Mary was not immaculate and that Jesus had brothers and sisters. All the basic concepts that children accept in the Catholic faith were simply considered stupid and untrue." She also learned to give a little. "I had a magnificent Latin teacher and one day she said, 'Well, my child, I understand your Latin was learned in the Church, but you must learn Cicero's Latin.' I looked at her with a sense of holding my own, but at the same time very curious and interested. Eventually, I admitted she was right."

Even her personal life, such as it was, fed into the "single line" of her development. She had friends but no intimate friends, though there were no intense hatreds, either. She simply wasn't very involved in the adolescent life of her schoolmates. They wanted a life-style and a future that she had already rejected. They were of another less-interesting world than the one she was sure she would find. "I wasn't interested in the kind of conversation about boys that implied you would shut yourself off in a house," she says. Not that she rejected the idea of marriage or children; she only knew that there would be another kind of purpose and activity in her life as well, though she wasn't very sure what it would be.

Even at McGill University, exploratory relationships with men did not fill important spaces, as they do in the lives of other young women. She did not go out on dates where the raison d'être for the evening is the date itself; he talks about himself, she talks about herself, while each checks an internal barometer for an indication of whether "that feeling" is likely to emerge. Madeleine's social life happened as an integral part of the things she did. "If you were involved with people in an activity, you went out with them after and had a coffee or a chat. I didn't see personal relationships as a separate thing. Questions of love and marriage weren't secondary, but they weren't primary, either. Only the activity was primary—the struggle."

The Activity; that's where the single line had led. She joined the Canadian Student Assembly, a militant activist group she had noticed for the first time during her freshman year when they had spoken out against fraternities and sororities. Madeleine had been getting the rush from the "top" sororities then, but she knew it was because she was a graduate of Trafalgar. The elitism clearly moved right through the university community and beyond, and she wanted no part of that, but it was the Student Assembly's campaign for 500 annual scholarships for working-class children that made her recognize their spirit as kin to her own. She joined their "struggle" and poured into it all the passion held in reserve since the loss of innocent saints. But in 1940 leftist groups were not exactly heralded in the streets of Quebec, and Madeleine was soon labelled as a communist, for the first but not the last time.

"My approach was not Marxist," she says, "I approached the issue of free scholarships as a militant reformist Catholic supporting the Dominican position. But there were repercussions anyway. We were threatened with expulsion from the university and I had to make a serious choice. Was this important enough to risk being called communist and maybe not graduate? I had fought the absolutism of the convent, but now I began to think of why there was such repression. If we were working for a just cause, why was this happening?"

In 1939-40 the secretary-treasurer of the Student Assembly went to China to visit Norman Bethune and Mao, who was then in the hills. When he returned, Madeleine was asked to find a speaker to introduce him at a public meeting. She couldn't find anyone. "I went from student leader to student leader and I was so *disgusted* with their *cowardice* that I came back and I said, 'I have been to the presidents of all the clubs and they are such *cowards* I wouldn't want to see them on our platform. *I* will be the speaker.' "

Her fists have clenched again and her voice has taken on that peculiar and effective razor-edged quality I first heard on the speaker's platform. "I was not a likely result of convent education," she says, but in fact, she was. Her abandoned religious passion had only changed its name and shape. "I had myself encouraged discussion at the Newman Club that made me question my religious beliefs more than I had done at Trafalgar, and I had studied sociology, which also helped place things in perspective. Catholic beliefs were hardly possible now. My faith went to people and, in particular, to workers."

She made the decision during her last year at McGill; she decided to dedicate her life to improving conditions for the working class. It was a social decision because she chose to repudiate her middle-class identity and take out membership among the working classes. It was also a political choice. I come to you from the inside, not the outside, she would be able to say in time. *I understand. You can trust me to know what is best, because I am one of you.*

She also cut off a relationship with a "liberally-minded" middle-class man. "I knew his life would be very different and that we'd never get along. I was going to be a union organizer, and a middle-class professional wasn't going to have a wife who would have arguments and battles and melees on the picket line and get thrown into jail. I knew the kind of personal relationship I might possibly develop with a man would be one that fitted in with that. The person would have to be a companion in those kinds of struggles."

Madeleine did graduate in 1940, and she spent the next year living at home and working as a free-lance activist, for lack of a better term, while looking for an opening as a union organizer. She also got married—to Valdimar Bjarnason, a student-worker activist from UBC who had moved to Montreal. The marriage didn't work. He went off to the war around 1942, and when he returned four years later, Madeleine was deeply involved in union work and it was too late. Typically, part of the romantic disenchantment was ideological. "I saw the struggle differently, I identified more with the struggle of Quebec workers; it was just not the kind of relationship that was relevant."

Generally, her friends and acquaintances thought her ambitions were crazy. Why would an upper-middle-class, convent-trained graduate of Trafalgar and McGill University want to join the hurly-burly, slightly disreputable world of labour organizing? They thought she was some sort of a freak, or worse, and that she'd get over it when she grew up. "Basically, it just wasn't permitted for a woman from that society to join the working class and their cause. You climbed *up* the social ladder, you didn't climb down, and I couldn't be forgiven for that." But there was a woman who encouraged her, one Lea Roback who was education director for the International Ladies Garment Workers Union. Lea did not think Madeleine was crazy. She said, "Why not?" and that was all Madeleine needed.

Her family supported her decision, too, as a matter of principle. They disagreed with her ideas, but they respected her integrity. Her grandfather had been a carpenter, had worked in the mines and run a grocery store; he had been involved with public welfare through the Church and was a staunch defender of Madeleine's freedom of choice. His support and that of her parents never faltered. They only worried that she'd go to jail, and warned her to be careful. Later, Duplessis made several attempts to use her parents against her, but he never succeeded; when she needed support in order to obtain release on bail, her mother deposited $2,000. Later on, when she was condemned for seditious conspiracy in the Lachute strike, her father was asked what he thought of his daughter's doings. "My daughter and I have different views about things," he replied, "but I respect her, and I know she's honest."

In 1942, Madeleine landed a job with the War Organizing Committee, as an office secretary, the only job open to a woman. But she learned fast, and within weeks she was talking to the workers, writing pamphlets, and distributing them in defiance of the anti-littering by-law, one of Duplessis' sillier anti-labour measures. She then became office secretary for the A. F. of L. War Labor Organizing Committee, where she met Kent Rowley, who wanted to organize the textile workers. Madeleine became associated with Rowley and on February 1, 1943, she took charge of organizing the workers of the Dominion Textile cotton mills in the St. Henri district of Montreal for the United Textile Workers of America (A. F. of L.). That was the real beginning.

In 1943 the conditions of Quebec textile workers were appalling. Children from the age of 10 worked 55 hours a week for as little as 18 cents an hour (in unionized war industries, 35 cents was a working hourly minimum). Most of the men worked 65 hours a week. There was no such thing as seniority; promotion depended on whom the foreman or boss liked that week. Women suffered most from favouritism since sex was a common trade-off—better jobs were available to women who slept with their male superiors—and they lived in fear of being pushed back to the hardest jobs on the worst machines. Children were punished or misused since it was assumed that an employer could behave "in loco parentis", and anyone of any age who used the bathroom more than twice a day had his pay docked. There was no lunch hour (workers ate at their machines) and no sick leave; there were no fire escapes, sprinklers, or ladders. (There are non-unionized needle-trade shops in Quebec today where immigrant women still work under similar conditions.)

Organizing Dominion Textile Mills was a baptism of fire for Madeleine that lasted four years. She visited workers in their homes and gained their confidence, convincing them that a union was the only answer. Being a woman was an advantage; other women trusted her to understand their problems on the job. And if a husband complained that unions were for men, his wife could always point at Madeleine. She had everyone's respect.

The majority of workers were signed up in a few months and all seemed well when the federal government duly granted certification rights; but Dominion Textile flatly refused to recognize the union. A strike seemed inevitable. But the A. F. of L. had committed itself not to strike during the war years. The new textile union would have been in defiance of the law and the A. F. of L., whose support they needed. There were meetings of 1500 people "screaming to strike" says Madeleine. "They had the strength necessary in themselves and as a group to do it, and to convince them that we couldn't, thought it was justified morally and tactically in the immediate sense, was a terrible task. I remember those scenes in the huge halls. People were screaming. We got some of the MLA's and other public figures to be with us on the platform, and some of the bureaucrats of the A. F. of L., and they would all wilt in fear and trembling before this violent crowd. I'd have to tell them I'd look after it."

In 1946 they struck—3000 workers in Montreal and 3000 in the Dominion Textile plant at Valleyfield, Quebec. The strike lasted 100 days. The company applied for and was granted an injunction that made picketing illegal, but the striking workers tore up the papers. Then in August the dramatic confrontation took place during which 6000 rocks were thrown. Rowley was arrested for inciting a riot and Madeleine took over. Reluctantly, the company agreed to accept the results of a vote to be held on the question of establishing the new union. But in September, on the eve of the secret balloting, Madeleine discovered that there was a warrant out for her arrest, charging her with attempting to bribe children into making false oaths at Rowley's trial. She went into hiding in Valleyfield workers' homes while the terms of the next day's vote were being negotiated and a runner went back and forth bringing her information and taking back her advice to the negotiating table. Then her lawyer went to the judge in Montreal, who said he'd let her off on $500 bail if she came before him. A trusted cab driver ran her into Montreal and the bail was negotiated.

At 9 p.m. she was back in Valleyfield where a big meeting had been called. "There were about 1000 people, the strikers and their mothers, wives, sons, and daughters. It was a triumphal meeting because the provincial police were still looking for me, and here I was on the platform saying I'd been bailed out. Then I denounced the whole thing; the false story about the kids. I told them it was to blacken the name of the union on the eve of the vote, and that we'd fought 100 days and nobody was going to be fooled. We were going to make sure between now and tomorrow night, when the votes were counted, that nobody robs us, because anybody who tries will get run out of town, that's all."

Facing me in the quiet of my living room, Madeleine seems electric with excitement as she relives that dramatic time. Her body appears tense, her muscles are taut, her face is animated, and her eyes flash with the remembered thrill of leadership and risk-taking and victory and, well, *power*, that's what it is; she is not immune.

"I phoned the government election officer about 10 p.m. and I said, 'I'm coming down to the hotel lobby and you be there, because we're going to re-negotiate the proceedings of the vote'. He protested that he was in bed and I said, 'You be in that lobby and I'll be there in 15 minutes. That's all you've got.' He was sitting in the lobby trying to look dignified, and he's got all of his men posted at a slight distance from him sitting around the lobby. The fellow striker and I moved in on him and he started to say, 'It's all settled' and I said, 'That's a lot of hogwash. You did what Duplessis told you to do, and Duplessis isn't going to get away with it. The only reason I was under arrest is so you can steal the vote, and it's not going to be stolen.' So we sat down and I told him how the vote would be conducted, and while he was protesting, about 300 women marched down to the front of the hotel led by Lea Duval, it was fantastic, this buxom woman with her flaming blond-red hair and they were singing victory songs, union songs, chanting my name, *Madeleine Parent, Madeleine Parent. . . .* "

An image of Jeanne d'Arc flashes across my mind, Jeanne leading *her* troops into *her* battles inspired by God-given visions. Madeleine emerges as her twentieth-century counterpart—as ready and as willing to be martyred. "Yes, I would die," she tells me. Her identification with the oppressed and the exploited has taken on the very religious absolutism she claims she fought at convent school. I begin to understand those famous portraits of medieval saints whose eyes are fixed on heaven. Heaven or earth, it's the fixation that counts.

"A terrible beauty is born," wrote Yeats in his "Easter 1916" poem about the Irish revolutionaries, and I have some of these same ambivalent feelings about the tiny, exciting woman seated across from me in my living room. I find myself objecting more to the rhetoric of her language (which hasn't changed since the thirties) than to the ideas she is expressing—after all, general approval for basic job security and fair wages is as entrenched in a liberal society as motherhood used to be. Rather, I am ill-at-ease with the blacks and whites of her language and the lack of nuance.

I wonder about her, and I think of the several people, a union worker, an NDP politician and an expert in labour law, who told me they felt she used the workers of Texpack in the strike of 1971 in order to make a point about American ownership in Canada (she is and always has been a militant nationalist). The workers won very little from that strike in pay increases, as Madeleine admits, and there was a lot of publicity about foreign ownership. But Madeleine denies the accusations—she has differentiated herself from other union leaders, she says, by *supporting* workers and refusing to join in cahoots with management.

But she does believe in highly-directive leadership. At a meeting of a Toronto local, one day, I watched her skillfully plant the idea of a strike without any prior suggestion from the membership. Later she said that union members must be prepared in advance; "Instead of saying to the workers, 'this is a problem, what should we do', I know from my years of experience how to second-guess management, and I tell our members. Our union has never failed to get the members to accept our recommendations, and that by secret ballot vote." It's certainly an efficient way to proceed, but watching and listening I am bothered by the assumption that the end justifies the means, a disturbing philosophy that may be applied in degrees that vary from an act of political extremism with world-wide repercussions to the simple manipulation of union members; a philosophy that can justify any action in the present by linking it to a hoped-for condition in the future.

Yet, I admire Madeleine's strength and her courage. To have been such a woman in Quebec in the forties and early fifties; to be called a witch, and to learn that school children are reciting prayers that you'll leave town; to walk by a schoolyard and watch the nuns hurry the children off the playground so they won't be polluted by your presence; to have to carry a birth certificate at all times to disprove the story that you're a Russian spy who was dropped on the east coast of Canada by a submarine; to be called a lesbian and accused of perverting women; and to affect the lives of others, such as the young organizer who had to postpone her marriage for a year because it was claimed that you had corrupted her. To survive all this, you need a special spirit. They didn't burn her at the stake, though in another age they would have. They only tried her for "seditious conspiracy".

Her stories come tumbling out. About how she incited the hatred of Duplessis by being unafraid the first time they met. And about the time she marched on the Quebec parliament with a union delegation and unwittingly interrupted Duplessis's birthday party when they trooped into the parliamentary dining room. Duplessis ordered the staff not to serve the union people lunch, but Madeleine set that right by telling the waiter she and her group would sit there overnight unless they got something to eat. She talks, of course, about her arrest and trial for seditious conspiracy during the bitter Lachute strike of 1947. Once again the accusation was that she was a communist, though, at that time, only Duplessis could say just what a communist was. As a result of that trial, Madeleine was convicted and sentenced to two years in Kingston penitentiary; but the court reporter died before his transcripts were complete and a new trial was ordered.

She and Rowley were not tried again until 1954. The long original trial had damaged them, but it had also damaged Duplessis as they had used the courtroom to repeat their accusations against the régime. "Every year we would come up to stand trial, and every year the crown prosecutor would say it was not in the public interest to proceed at this time. Finally in 1954, Judge Caron was on the bench. He could see the whole thing. The prosecutor had a letter from Duplessis saying the trial wasn't in the public interest, but Caron insisted on seeing it and with a contemptuous gesture he threw it back and said, 'We will now proceed.' The prosecutor refused to make any proof against us, so Caron told the jury they had no choice but to acquit us. So they did and it was over. Just like that—seven years later."

My favourite story is the kidnapping because it typifies her reckless, daring spirit, her thrill in power, and the exaltation of being on the side of the angels. It concerns the events leading up to the notorious "expulsion" of Parent and Rowley from the A. F. of L., on the grounds that they were communists.

In 1945 Parent and Rowley learned that A. F. of L. international president, Tony Valente, had been invited to Quebec City to meet with labour minister Antonio Barrette. They also learned that representatives of the Dominion Textile Company were to be at the meeting and that Valente would be offered a contract with a union check-off (union dues taken off an employee's pay by the company and remitted to the union) on condition that he fire Madeleine and Kent Rowley. "That contract would not have been negotiated by the workers," says Madeleine, "so we decided that I would go to the Montreal station and wait for Valente as he changed trains from Washington. There was a government man there waiting to escort him to Quebec City, but as soon as Valente came up the escalator, we grabbed him. I said, 'You're coming with me to the Windsor Hotel. You're not going to make a deal, and if you do you'll be denounced and the whole thing will fall apart because you won't have any members.' So he agreed to come with me and he became my captive in a hotel.

"We kept him there for as long as he stayed in Montreal—a full day, I think—and I'd answer the telephone when one of the management executives called for him. Barrette called and I said, 'Yes, Mr. Barrette, he'll talk to you'. Valente was very careful when he spoke. He said, 'Well, I'll ask her'—he knew who was making the decisions. So there was no deal, and he went back home."

There were other confrontations between the radical textile union and the parent A. F. of L. during the next years, so nobody was really surprised when the crunch came in 1952, at the height of the cold war, and Parent and Rowley were fired. Lloyd Klennert, the secretary-treasurer of the United

Textile Workers of America, came in from Washington to do the job personally. When Madeleine and Kent entered their office that morning, they found that it had been sacked and that full file drawers were missing.

Sam Baron of the United Textile Workers of America was brought in as Canadian director of the union and Parent and Rowley left—finally. But Madeleine kept her office in Montreal, (Sam Baron had to take his headquarters elsewhere) trying to convince her contacts in the mills that a victory of the Catholic unions in Quebec would be better for them than the A. F. of L. (The original Catholic syndicates lost their denominational character and evolved into the present Confederation of National Trade Unions.) Madeleine tried to reorganize, but was unsuccessful. Finally in 1967, after 15 "difficult years" as she puts it, the office was moved to Brantford, Ontario to reorganize there as the Canadian Textile and Chemical Union, a small all-Canadian conglomerate that has made them more enemies than friends in the Canadian Labour Congress, but has undoubtedly influenced thinking about international unions in Canada.

Madeleine has woven her personal experience throughout a lifetime of action, commitment, and risk. Her divorce from Valdimar Bjarnason didn't happen until 1951, because "the time wasn't right". Divorce, like marriage itself, like any personal event, had to be squeezed in between crises; and divorce, in particular, had to be handled delicately, especially among the Catholic union membership in Quebec. The relationship with Rowley developed naturally over the years. "We were companions in all our struggles and we respected each other. He was the first man to ask me to organize and when I said, 'Do you think I can do it?' even though it was the only thing on earth I wanted to do, he said, 'Of course you can, as well as anybody else. There's nothing you cannot do.' Kent isn't afraid to stand alone, and having stood alone myself so often as a child, I recognized and understood that ability."

Madeleine was 35 when they married in 1953, and they thought they might have a child, "if it could be worked in with the struggle". She even got as far as a visit to the gynecologist, who recommended rest and vitamins in preparation for pregnancy, but then Harding Carpets went on strike and that was the end of that.

Madeleine and Kent Rowley have led some of the more bitter strikes of recent years—Texpack in Brantford in 1971 and Artistic Woodwork in Toronto in 1973. Madeleine would prefer not to compromise. The desired state is not just better economic conditions for workers in a capitalist society, but a society where workers control production. For this belief, and because of their radical-nationalist views, she and Rowley have been effectively ostracized from the CLC.

She's been called unscrupulous and power-hungry and a lot of other things, but there are others—young people on the left, for instance—who have thoroughly committed themselves to her and whatever she does. The enormous support her strike at Artistic Woodwork drew was not unconnected with the strength of her personality. And to those who knew Madeleine in Quebec during the darker moments of the Duplessis era she remains an epic heroine, a sort of superwoman who wasn't afraid to lead her troops into fires, and usually got them out safely on the other side.

She continues to work on behalf of the powerless, organizing immigrant women in the textile trades in particular. The terror of being buried alive at the age of six has never dissipated. It prowls along behind her in the shadow, nipping sharply at her heels. Neither anger nor passion has failed her, and she's surviving mightily, I'd say, looking about for fires to march through. History may answer those who claim she tends to light the fires herself then pour gasoline on the flames, but in the meantime she endures, as charismatic and as strong a woman as this Canadian century has known.

Rita MacNeil:
Singing It Like It Is

BY MYRNA KOSTASH

In March 1972, a group of us were planning, a "feminist extravaganza" at the University of Toronto, and someone suggested we invite Rita MacNeil to sing. I'd never heard of her, but I was delegated to call her on the phone. She had a soft, infinitely sweet, lilting, and polite voice and she agreed without hesitation, almost as if she weren't shy at all, to come sing for us. We put her at the end of the evening, after the all-woman string quartet, the feminist plays, and the karate demonstration.

We couldn't have planned it better. By the time she hit her last, remarkable note, we were all in tears. We jumped up and down and clapped, laughed and wept, yelled and hugged each other. She had done for me, for one, what nothing and no one else had done, not even the Chicago Women's Liberation Rock Band: bridged the chasm between the rhetoric and sensation of sisterhood.

I remember that she sang unaccompanied, just her own clear, pure, still voice and her hands clapping, her body bouncing and swaying, her eyes closed, and her face a moving picture of expressions ranging from wryness to vulnerability. But it was the songs themselves which stirred me up, a combination of ballad, blues, gospel and what I can only think of as "union" songs—the music that labour militants sang in their picket lines to keep up their courage as the police advanced. I suppose it was the sentimental identification, through such

music, with the generations of rebels who had preceded this feminist generation of mine which moved me most. She sang, with a hypnotic body rhythm and with high notes that sent shivers along my skin, about the contents of my female life—girlhood, love, madness, dreams, family—and somehow endowed them with the urgency of a mass protest that I was committed to, right there, with all the women. It was unforgettable.

She is my age, thirty. That is about all we have in common. Yet it is one of the mysteries of the women's movement that she and I have come together and understood each other. This is her story, as I tell it.

Etobicoke is a suburb located somewhere in western Toronto. If you travel there by subway, it is impossible to know for sure where it lies in relation to the city you do know. It is Out There, at the end of the subway line, and there is absolutely no reason to go there. Like Scarborough, Don Mills, and Mississauga, it is a region which, like all such territories, will always lie on the outskirts of metropolitan energy. Thus it was that I had been living four years in Toronto before I set foot in Etobicoke. It was to meet Rita MacNeil.

At the Islington subway station you board a Number 38 bus that will take you to Horner Street and Brown's Line, which is where you will get off. The passage en route is uninspiring and emphasizes the dreary isolation in which the housewives live, in the rows of brick bungalows trimmed in red and pink and green on streets like Inverness, Belvia, and Maybrook, and the forlorn cement spaces in which the husbands work, Consolidated-Bathurst Packaging, Standard Tube Canada Ltd., National Silicates Ltd. The bus goes past railway yards, over the Queen Elizabeth Way, past construction sites and warehouses and turns at Horner Street, where Rita's and

David's house, salmon-pink with a sloping red roof and two trees by the front door, stands on a street like all the others. It has taken an hour to get here. To leave it to go anywhere would be a major undertaking. How many housewives can get away?

Inside, it feels warm. They worked hard on this house, after a near-defeat on a ramshackle farm, and their careful, respectful touch is evident in the pine cupboards, the antique clock and mirror, the red broadloom and cheerful wallpaper. It is, in spite of Rita's protestations to the contrary, neat and tidy; not fanatically so, but neater than my place, for instance. When the sun shines through the kitchen windows, it is in fact charming. Four-year-old Wade, a beautiful boy with huge dark eyes, a flirtatious smile and quick wit, waltzes through the rooms in a happy mood. Six-year-old Laura, home from school for lunch, moves quietly and sedately, looking up at me with serious eyes that suggest behind them a world of unsuspected gravity. Rita presides at the kitchen table, her heavy body wrapped loosely in a robe.

The kitchen was the forum for my interviews with Rita. We would sit at the table drinking tea and sometimes beer, and she must have said, half a dozen times, how glad she was that I was a journalist who was a feminist. I had the impression that, otherwise, she would not open up: as she implied, journalists "screw" you, it's their trade. Feminists, on the other hand, trade in sympathy, kindness, and support. That observation set the tone of our conversations. And conversations they were, for she was the rare kind of interviewee who asked the interviewer questions and was interested in the answers. We were like next-door neighbours having a consciousness-raising rap, and if we couldn't be nice with each other, then we couldn't be anything at all.

Her life has been so unlike mine I didn't know where to begin to make the connections. And her character, trusting, generous, co-operative, and yet—I couldn't help thinking—fragile and only temporarily in control of more violent feelings, was so different from my own business-like reasonableness that I felt like an ox in an egg factory. And yet I knew what she was talking about, as she talked about where she had come from and what she had done. Maybe it was because she told it without cunning or subterfuge; you had to be dismally egocentric not to understand.

The last time I visited her, she said she was going alone to spend the summer back home, in Cape Breton. She was going to write songs and collect her father's poems and songs and live quietly in a little cottage by the sea. She loves it there; it is probably the only place she has loved, and she lives her life in this kitchen in suburban Toronto like a displaced person. She has been, in fact, displaced from practically everything she longs for; but a year from now I won't be able to say that any more. She's finding her way again and she was unwinding the journey, bit by bit, like a thin copper wire along the tabletop.

"The grass I thought was the greenest green
    Has more yellow than I've ever seen.
    And even the water's slowly turning brown.
    . . .
    I've only circled back to find
    Many changes made by time,
    And many changes in my mind.
    I was looking for a place called home."

Life after the age of eight was no longer simple. That was the year, 1952, that the MacNeils, all ten of them, left Big Pond, a peaceful and friendly village twenty-five miles from Sydney and the home of Rita's great-grandparents. They relocated in Sydney, in working-class Sydney, where father MacNeil got a job as a carpenter. He was, and is, a master carpenter. But somehow the money he earned never seemed enough. Eight children's mouths to feed, second-hand school uniforms, empty cupboards by Thursday morning, and only the crudest operations on Rita's harelip, with a weekly blessing upon it from the priest.

It was on her mother, in particular, that the constriction and insecurity of such a life weighed heavily.

When Rita speaks of something painful, she rocks. Her body becomes a rhythm, a rocking accompaniment to the beat of the sadness in her mind. She moves slowly back and forth in her chair and talks about her mother, Renee. Her voice is low, it drops, she looks down at her hands and the ache of her longing for her mother, now dead, is something I feel I could twist between my fingers. "I felt for her then, even though I didn't know what it was. I felt for her like you wouldn't believe. What a wasted life. She was never very happy. And, then, when she got sick, I would catch her by the window, looking out and crying. She was in no position to leave but, oh, I can just imagine how many times she must have wanted to."

It is, in fact, a commonplace female story. A young girl marries. Eight children. The colossal monotony of housework and childcare. Marital disillusion. Stuck inside the walls of home, until one day she is too frightened to go outside any more. Not to mention the daily struggles with the wage-packet, how far it can go, the eventual regret for an education that was never expected, where *you* came from you never got such a ticket out, the fear that the children might have to repeat all this for yet another generation, there must be something they can do differently. A good, sweet, silent daughter who observes and takes it all in, loves her mother to distraction, knowing she is the bedrock of the family on whom they all make impossible demands for support, knowing that there is nothing that she, little girl, can do to help. It wasn't until years later that Rita learned to love her father this way, too. She sees now that he had no life either, and so there is no one to blame. The only thing that is important now is to see that "we were poor in lots of ways, but rich in others". And that these parents were "pretty darn good to raise eight of us, all proud, sensitive, productive people".

Rita's photo album is full of pictures of babies and children. Her own, Laura and Wade. Near the front, her mother sits on the edge of a pink bed holding baby Laura. Renee is wearing a pretty blue dress and the curve of her eyebrow, the streak of her smile and the thick brown hair sweeping up from her high forehead show me she was beautiful. On the next page she is there again, with Laura several months older, but this time Renee's face is white and strained, the smile is tentative, her body stiffer. Now I see something of her unhappiness, and of the cancer which killed her four years later. She is wearing a sleeveless white dress. At her funeral, there would be four hundred people. And Rita would sing her a song, one hand on the coffin.

> "Renee wore a dress of white
> White was her colour.
> And on her face she wore a smile
> I've seen on no other.
>
> . . .
>
> And the life she led and the dreams she had
> Were like so many another.
> Renee in your dress of white
> It soon would change its colour."

It wasn't until Rita was thirteen that extensive surgery on her lip was undertaken. Until then, and even after, she lived shyly and diffidently, wary of people's mockery and unkindness. The operations kept her out of school, and the struggle to catch up with her peer group after that was difficult. "It was a hell of a job later to get me back into a grade that would suit my age and height. I was real backward. And so emotionally striken because I was so different. I struggled through somehow. God, I was so dumb. But I really tried. And by grade nine I led the class in History and Science." She was, she says, "pathetically religious". It helped her struggle, however, in that it made her want desperately to be "good". To gratify her teachers, pacify her parents, and to please God. At one point, she thought of joining the Sisters of the Good Shepherd; the additional restrictions of a cloistered order would be extra pleasing to God. But her older sister, a nun at the time, encouraged her to see and do more before making such a commitment. When Rita did make up her mind, it was to run away to Toronto.

In the meantime, she nourished herself with music. It is her passion, her joy, her life. As a girl, she'd listen constantly to the radio and the songs she heard would "release a lot of feelings. It would ease my mind. Looking back, I can see that I wouldn't have been able to get through a lot of things without music." She would learn the songs—folk, pop, gospel, Country and Western, blues—and sing them at home to herself and then to her parents. Her mother was excited. "From the first time I sang, she wanted me to be a singer. I can truly say she was the only one who really believed then in my singing. She had great hopes that one day I would blossom out. She put all her chips on me."

The fact was that her mother didn't want her and her sisters to marry—she cried when they did—and the fantasy-prospect of a daughter who would grow up to be independent and rewarded because of the gift of her voice and the touching message of her songs was exciting indeed. It was an alternative to female inevitability. Rita, at least, could leave working-class Sydney with its adolescent marriages, unexpected pregnancies, numbed workingmen, stir-crazy housewives, and bewildered children. So Rita went to singing lessons; and the teacher would sing but Rita, unbearably shy, stayed silent. Scared of opening her mouth and displeasing her audience, in spite of the clear soprano welling in her throat. She did sing a couple of times in the local Kiwanis Festivals, but she broke down half-way through the song and cried all the way home. She didn't sing in public again until 1971 when she joined the women's liberation movement.

"You know, my friend told me that
her mind died.
To stand alone she could not survive.
. . .
Oh won't you take the time to free your minds
Have you got a friend, has her mind died?"

Rita finished grade eleven in Sydney and then split. She had
failed the French course, and in Nova Scotia in those days if
you failed one subject you had to repeat the whole year. The
prospect was galling. So she went to Toronto, Gotham City.
Job. Money. At home you were so sick of being poor you could
only think of running off to Silver City. Her mother supported
her in this, cherishing the dream that in Toronto Rita would
become a nightclub singer. Music. Money. Freedom. She, too,
had once worked in Toronto, at Eaton's, and had had money
all of her own. The taste of it was still sweet in her memory.
She told Rita to go.

Rita lasted only one summer as a file clerk at the CNR. Then
summer ran out and Rita with it. Back home again, she
worked as a housekeeper—"the story of my life"—for a woman
expecting her sixth child. She worked from eight in the morning to nine at night, every day except Sunday, for twelve
dollars a week. She gave her wages to her parents. "That
woman expected a hell of a lot for twelve dollars, that's all I
can say. Five kids, the house a real mess, real dirty. My parents
were so embarrassed. They hated me doing that, cleaning up
other people's dirt."

It's no wonder that the irony of "liberated" career women
hiring housekeepers to allow themselves freedom to pursue jobs
away from home made her smile. They would hire someone
like her. Sturdy, dependable, and proud of her hard work—and
who would take two dollars an hour as the going rate. It was
never so much the housework in these houses that galled
Rita—although *any* housekeeping, even her own, bores her
silly—but the fact that it paid so little; by their token wages,

even these middle-class female employers acknowledged that the work she did was deemed unimportant and undeserving of much respect. Women's work.

Back in Toronto that same fall, Rita summoned up all her courage to go apply for jobs and ended up in the personnel room at Eaton's. She was hired as a switchboard operator, answering customers' complaints and credit enquiries. The "phones bouncing off the walls", she burst into tears. Instead of being fired, she was comforted. It was an office full of women.

She was nineteen and she cleared forty-seven dollars a week and thought she was really living. Ashamed now, she tells me that she blew most of her money on junk clothes and shoes that pinched. Today, to be able to have some money of her own, and time away from home, she works three hours a day as a janitor at the local movie theatre. None of this is what her mother envisaged. "Oh, I wish I had done things differently, all of it. Been smarter. I had no idea of women's liberation in those days, believe me. I wouldn't do again any of what I did then. I would have educated myself better. I wouldn't have got pregnant . . . . But I didn't know much then. And I'm still learning." Still, it's money of her own. With it, she paid for more operations on her lip and nose. With it, she can plan to leave her husband and home. She can even laugh: "I was at work, in my t-shirt and jeans, and the size of me, with a broom sweeping, fourteen garbage bags of dirt and popcorn boxes, my back was breaking after that, and I'm singing, 'Getting Away From It All'. I laughed and laughed and laughed. It felt good."

For the life of me, I can't see what's so funny. In almost every way, the details of her life depress and enrage me, and here she sits laughing—and I'm laughing too and I'm glad we are, even if I can't understand it, because the alternative is unbearable, is too heavy, as she says, like it's some kind of big joke that she should be standing with a broom, her body spilling out over the waistband of her jeans, her son playing among the seats with torn upholstery, her voice swelling above the stage curtains—so this is what she's come to, eleven years after leaving her mother's house. Real funny.

There was a time she took herself more seriously. When she was working at Eaton's she took singing lessons, and with the new confidence inspired by surviving well enough on her own in the big city, she opened her mouth and let it out. She became disciplined, confident, and professional under the tutelage of an enthusiastic teacher who encouraged her to explore, in gesture and inflection, the emotional range of the music she so strongly identified with: blues and gospel. And she had a taste of what she wanted. One night a gang of them from work went to the Colonial Tavern and persuaded her to sing for the crowd. She got a standing ovation and someone passed the hat. She sang that night "The Wild Colonial Boy" and "Ramblin' Rose". "They all near went crazy for me. They all stood up and started shouting and screaming. Getting that kind of reaction from an audience is a real high."

When Rita talks now about that period, about her first real accomplishment, she becomes animated, her face lifts, her hands fly about, her voice rises, she becomes the person implied behind the lovely notes and assertive lyrics of her songs. "I was singing, besides blues and spirituals, songs like 'I Feel Pretty' and 'I Enjoy Being a Girl'. Oh wow. But I had a lot of people excited about me. I *was* good then, I've got to admit it. I had a hell of a range and, boy, I could belt them out. I could do them like you wouldn't believe. I *love* the blues. I could get you down on your knees with some of them. I went to lessons for two years and had a hundred songs down pat and then my teacher was ready to bring agents in. She said I was ready for the clubs, that I could become a well-paid entertainer, that I could make it. I wish it had happened. I would have loved it. I had long black hair and weighed 118 pounds. I was feeling confident. I had nice clothes, low-cut gowns. I wasn't bad then, why not say it? I was pretty damn good. I was scared, sure. But people who heard me knew I had something. Too much is right. You'd better believe too much." What happened instead is that Rita got pregnant and her life curled up on itself.

Rita and her friends would go, Friday evenings, to the Maritime Club dances. There, in 1965, she met a young Italian called Philip. He worked in a shoe factory and, although she saw him every weekend for three years, she never met his family. He was a Sicilian through and through. He would never marry her, there was a young woman in Italy promised to him, his family would never tolerate his serious approaches to another. So they would go to Oshawa to dance, to avoid meeting anyone he knew. It wasn't the most flamboyant of courtships, but she was in love. "I was terribly in love. I still maintain that I was. Deeply. And he was too, even though it took him three years to admit it. I have no bad feelings about the relationship. I really loved him."

She was a virgin when she met him, and two years later she still was. She "held out" from fear, from disgust. Not that she was afraid of becoming pregnant—she wasn't sure how that took place. She had learned at home and at church that sex, whatever it was, was filthy and sinful. She was "pretty dumb", she says, totally ignorant, believing at age nineteen that babies were born out of the mother's navel. "Nobody had ever told me different. I told you I was 'good'," she laughs self-mockingly. No one spoke of sex at home, it was considered a terrible thing to know, especially for the women, and if she brought it up with her mother, she would "cringe in the corner".

Eventually, Philip threatened to leave her for someone "easier". Terrified and disconsolate, Rita collapsed. She could not stop crying, shaking, or vomiting. She went to work crying. They put her in the infirmary for a day, laden with sedative. A girlfriend called Philip and he was reconciled. Then they made love. You could count on the fingers of both hands how many times they made love. Then she got pregnant.

In the mornings, she felt sick. Puzzled, she went to her sister's doctor, a Roman Catholic, who told her what the matter was. She asked him if there was anything that could be done, to stop it. He frowned: definitely not. He told her to go through with it and then give the baby up. She walked home dumb-founded, humiliated, terrified. She wanted to commit suicide. At least it would wipe out the shame that now lay, not only on her, but on her family as well. She told Philip. He said he couldn't marry her, but he would try to get her an abortion. They went to another doctor, their last hope. He told them they were immoral.

Philip offered to kick her in the stomach or to push her from a moving car. She tried laxatives. He bought her a box of Keene's dry mustard which, according to old tales, would abort you if you put it in your bathwater and sat in it. She never used it. But her sister found it and called the police, telling them that her sister and her sister's lover were plotting an abortion. One morning, when Philip was with her, the police arrived and warned them that abortion was illegal and they could get into trouble. That more or less scared Philip off. But, as Rita points out, it wasn't as if he hadn't tried.

Her sister then showed her the *Life* magazine pictures of human fetuses, and called her parents. When her mother arrived, Rita, shaken by guilt, half-convinced she had contemplated murder, agreed to go back home. "I never saw Philip again. He called me up just before I went back to Nova Scotia and told me he loved me and would we ever see each other again. He broke down and cried and said he didn't know what to do. My sister grabbed the phone and said, 'You ugly bastard, what you did to my sister, you wouldn't want to happen to your sister.' They didn't blame me because they didn't think I knew what I was doing. I didn't. But I knew I loved somebody."

At home again, Rita was comforted and supported, not hidden away, by her family (she even sang once at a priests' gathering) and she renewed her Catholic faith—"I was 'good' again"—so that under the combined pressures of charity and confession, she agreed to keep her baby and, even, once Laura was born, became her defender, sleeping as she did with one hand in the cradle as if protecting her from Philip (she thinks now) who had so badly wanted the abortion. But it was not really a conciliatory experience. She was sick throughout the pregnancy, in labour for three days when she should have had a Caesarian, and, after the delivery, her dismay at her ravaged body threw her into despair. "And I bawled and I cried, bawled and cried. It shook my whole being up. I just wanted to get out of there." She left Laura with her mother and went back to Toronto.

The experience put a harsh twist in her life which has never really completely straightened out. She never regained her original weight or figure, a catastrophe that threatened more than simple vanity, terminating as it did the dream of becoming a nightclub singer; you can't get promoted looking fat and sounding wheezy. But it was more than her body that held her back now. After such a brief escape from them, she was caught again in the traps of self-doubt, guilt, and insecurity. In such mental shape, how could she really believe she could pull off such a fantasy? What right had she to dream she could get more out of life than a measly pay cheque from Eaton's?

She was a broken person, then, she says. She had lost almost everything. It was no real surprise that four years later she would be singing her heart out at a mass demonstration to repeal the abortion laws. It would be the second time her life had been turned on its head.

Back in Toronto, she met David Langham at a party and three months later they were married. It was not a difficult decision to make. "I married him to give Laura a name. And then, thinking of my poor mother taking care of my daughter while I went to parties. *I* should have been taking care of her, but *how* was I going to take care of her? I could have done if I had been a feminist, but instead I saw David as security, he was fun and alive, and he loved me." And she loved him—not as she had done Philip, for that happened only once in life, but warmly and steadily, with respect and admiration. "David is great, he really is. There's no doubt about it." He is kind and mild, with the soft accent of his Yorkshire homeland and the manners of a reasonable and tender man. He is a draughtsman who enjoys his work, a settled personality pleased with his position in life. For a while, he was very good for Rita. But it was only a matter of time before her relief and gratitude ran out, leaving her face to face with her own chagrin.

Their plan was to live in the country, raising horses. They bought a delapidated 78-acre farm in Dundalk, 70 miles from Toronto, and started off with an old work horse. While David continued to work in the city, driving the 140-mile round trip every day, Rita tried to "make do" on the farm, in an old house without plumbing or heating, and to figure out "why I wasn't a happily married woman, like in the songs, with this fine man who was my husband. I was supposed to be mother, wife, cook, cleaner on this farm, trying to make everybody else happy, and wondering why the hell *I* was so unhappy. I've always been known to accept a lot of things, to keep the peace. I wasn't a women's liberationist in those days. Didn't know anything about my self-worth. Somewhere along the line my head was neglected—the house became my whole world. I really didn't have much choice; I was in it seven days a week." That was one thing; for another, she was lonely. For another, she got pregnant again and became very ill, "vomiting all over the place, rushing to and from hospitals for an intravenous. So that's what did it. I was useless. Couldn't do any work." So they sold the farm and moved back into the city. It had been a fruitless interlude.

The delivery of Wade, however, was a happy experience. An

easier birth. A wanted child. A beautiful child. Her relationship with her son is warm and open, incredibly loving, and gentle. And Wade is happy, a laughing child, direct and trusting with strangers, the way all children should be, in the best of possible worlds.

> "And the weeds they grow in the very
> back row
> Behind the tulip bed.
> And it was sad to find that after a time
> They grew inside her head."

She has a green fridge, a cat with a magnificent white coat, and we are drinking beer. She tells me that this house is a cage. "It seems to me I've just jumped from cage to cage to cage, if you know what I mean. I've got the feeling to go, fly off. I need to bloom so bad. I want to be free. But I'm scared. I'm finding excuses not to do it." Do it! I slam my fist on the table. We laugh. She has spoken with a combination of resignation and defiance. I don't know which feeling unbalances the other. Neither, I guess, does she.

Her cage. She has caught me off balance. I had imagined her otherwise and now she tells me she is trapped. I have read about these things. In the course of five years of feminist study, hundreds of testimonials came my way from middle-class and not so middle-class housewives lined up in their monotonous rows across the nation, bitterly shaking their brooms and eggbeaters as emblems of servitude they had always known was onerous but have only now publicly described that way. Feminists listened to the aggrieved mutter from the domestic front and concluded that it was husband and children who weighed so heavily upon these sisters, turning housewives into subversives. Smash monogamy? Trouble was, while it was certainly true that many women are entrapped by the dual tyrannies of selfish men and helpless children, there were also women, with the best of husbands and the sweetest of kids, who were climbing the walls.

And so Rita caught me off-balance. "You know, my three sisters keep pointing out that I have this wonderful husband. What the hell has that got to do with *my* personal being?" And so one has the impression that even if the adjustments and compromises were infinite—"Here, dear, let *me* do the laundry for a change. Put the kids into daycare. Take a night school course. Go home for a holiday. Lose weight. Take the day off. Tell me what's bothering you"—the sour, tough core of the woman's protest would remain untouched. Herein a mystery. What is ailing the women?

"I'm just like a scared kid, for heaven's sake. I don't know what I'm hiding from. I guess it started with the death of my mother in October, 1972. I started to slow down a lot, to think about life a lot, eh? I don't know, maybe I just want to. . . . It's really getting to me. I've been in this house for months and months and I'm scared to go out. Just like my mother. And I hate housework. Last Saturday, David did the laundry from one o'clock to ten o'clock. A month's worth. I refused to do it, let it pile up and up. He really does think I shouldn't have to do all the shitwork all the time. But *I'm* the one who's here all day. I used to be a real housekeeper—you could eat off my floors. But like the woman in *Homemaker's Digest* said, who the hell eats off your floors, anyway? So get out and do something. Yes, experience other things. Other relationships. Sure, that's what to do. But God, how?" She was to say later how much of what she had said struck her like a suicide note.

"When I was a young girl we used to play war
  In the back of Angus Anthony's store.
  . . .
  The girls played the Indians for we had believed
  They were the mindless, inferior breed.
  And the boys shot us down—one, two, three—
  As they danced around in their victory."

We sit at the table, exchanging stories of how we became feminists. Rita is easier now with the tape recorder, looks directly at me as she speaks, her hands relaxed in front of her instead of fussing with bits of tin foil and plastic that make a horrible, ear-jarring sound on the tape when I play it back. We both get excited, interrupt each other, our voices rise, we laugh. We're talking about something that makes us livelier than we've been for days. To use an analogy, we are talking about a revelation. We both confess to having encountered Women's Liberation on our own roads to Damascus: the encounter profoundly altered the route we were taking. And we don't see any way of ever going back.

"I had a friend who was going to meetings of the Toronto Women's Caucus, in 1971. She was telling me about it at a friend's house and the others were laughing about it. But I don't laugh at people. I remember her talking about the Abortion Caravan that went to Ottawa and everybody was laughing and then she talked about a demonstration at City Hall and how a bunch of businessmen booed at them and everybody there in the room thought that was terrific. Crazy women. And that really struck me. Real bad. That women get put down so much. So I went with her to a meeting. I didn't laugh at the idea. I've never laughed at anything to do with women. My friend was serious about it, so involved in it, I thought it must be important. I thought, I'm a woman."

In a way, it was inevitable that Rita should become a feminist. Her life until then was a kind of unconscious preparation for it, beginning with her agonized identification with her mother's unhappiness and ending with her own deep depression in the Etobicoke "cage". And in between the two extremes was a series of encounters with women which were the most secure and most valuable of her relationships: the nuns and students at her all-girl high school, her co-workers at Eaton's, her singing teacher, her girlfriends in Toronto, her older sister back home. She was positively ripe for a "sorority" that would define publicly the confused and guilty feelings she endured in private. Whoever, or whatever, could name her complaint would win her.

"Oh my goodness, I'll never forget when I walked in there, I was so scared. I didn't go out much or do many things, and this whole roomful of angry women is something I'd never been in before. Oh God, I'll never forget. It was so exciting. I came out of there all fired up. That sounds so stupid. Oh dear. It's like, before that I was one thing and after it something else." She laughs. The fact is, they were talking about abortion.

"They were talking about the demonstration in Ottawa and how nobody had come out to meet them. The *fire* in these women! I'd just never seen anything like it. Oh, it was just so beautiful. I couldn't believe there was so much power in women." Nor could she believe that they had come together to talk and do something about abortion on demand, the one issue most likely to hook her. Within the Movement, she finally had her chance to grapple in an organized and political way with the tenterhooks of her bitterness.

After the first meeting, she went home, sat down in the living room, and wrote a song. Where it came from, she doesn't know. Except, of course, that it came from her consistent love for music, the one form in which she had always found her speech, from the songs she sang herself at home and at work, from the songs her mother sang, and from this sudden and urgent need to record her exhilaration at finding the key to her recovery.

"So I decided to get involved. I would take the streetcar or walk to Adelaide Street. But I wouldn't speak out at meetings. Fifty articulate women! But eventually I realized how they felt about women, that they were fighting for women to get together. I could *sing* what I was feeling. So I asked if it would be all right if I sang for them. Oh yes! I was scared to death. Sure, it surprised me that I had a song. After all those years, that I had written a song. But before that meeting, what was I going to write about? 'I love him and he loves me, Oh how happy we can be'?" The song she wrote was "Need for Restoration".

> "So I found me a man in the good old tradition
> Being conditioned as I was.
> But when it came down to making big decisions
> I found he overlooked my mind.
> And there was unrest and a need for restoration
> To fill the needs in me."

In due course, Rita MacNeil became an integral part of the Toronto women's liberation movement. Where feminists gathered, to protest, demonstrate, celebrate, there was Rita, in the sun, the wind, and the rain with banners flapping around her, singing against the hostility and jeers of passers-by, whipping up the energy and solidarity of the women, spreading out over those who would listen the glory of her voice joined with the momentum of her courage in letting it all out, telling her story, describing the rage and the pain, reviewing the growth of sisterhood and feminist politics, so that no woman who heard her could stay unmoved. Along with her own voice she had found one for all of us.

"All I needed was more meetings and the response from the women to keep on writing. They would talk about the songs, they pushed me all the way, gave me support. It was phenomenal. The positive response from women who heard me was overwhelming. When I sing, I'm quite a different person. I come right out of myself. I'm glad to be involved with women. Hell, if I'm going to do anything with my life, that's where I want to do it."

Her songs are about her mother and her brother and her sisters, about going home, about a woman friend whose mind has died, about the loss of girlhood dreams and simple love, about the household trap, about her hatred of war and the historic lies about women, about exhaustion and discouragement in the struggle for self-realization and collective liberation. They are angry, ironic, sarcastic, sorrowful, poignant songs that encompass almost the entire experience of becoming a feminist. She is our troubadour. The irony of it all is that her confessions of pain make the rest of us exuberant. "I've never been able to figure it out. People get so high when they hear me sing—meanwhile I'm cutting my heart out."

Those were the intoxicating days of the movement: women emerging from their cocoons of private disillusion, from families, marriages, love affairs, from kitchens, offices, classrooms, to sit around in circles, saying, this is what happened to me and this is how I feel about it, answering, oh me too, me too, catching each other by the hand and shoulder, what does it mean? reading and analyzing it, maybe it's this and that. Falling into place. There was nothing on earth like that wide-eyed amazement and that stupendous relief at learning *you* were not the problem, you, lady, were not crazy or paranoid or frigid or schizophrenic. That you were not alone. That there were others like you, but stronger, braver, surer, who wanted to help you heal your wounds inside the clinic of sisterly politics. It was your last chance. You took it.

"Without Women's Liberation, I wouldn't be able to get through many a day. There *is* a way out, there *is* help and support. I just know I'll come out of it. I know I won't sit around for too much longer. And it's shown me a whole other side of myself. The reason a lot of women don't become feminists is that it does uproot you, totally. There's not many marriages that can survive that." For Rita, feminism meant two things: a get-away, and a paralysis. "After consciousness-raising, what? That's what I've been asking myself."

At first it was liberating to have a view of the world that described the "absurdities" of your own life. But, ultimately, of course, it required that action be taken to rectify at least the most glaring abuses, and it was at this point that Rita got stuck. Partly it had to do with the direction that the women's movement had taken. The Caucus had broken up into a myriad of theoretical grouplets and action projects, there was no single office or executive which represented the totality of feminist organization and the large collective in which Rita, and many others, had formerly met to share observations and insights had now split into sometimes antagonistic small groups debating along Marxist or Radical Feminist lines. This was an intellectual development which automatically excluded Rita, who felt she had nothing now to contribute: "I certainly felt at that time that women's liberation had become a middle-class movement. I felt I didn't have anything to say because there wasn't that old feeling of coming together. The women were a lot younger. I didn't think they were very interested in hearing how you couldn't get out of the house."

Whenever she was invited to sing, however, she would always go (and the invitations started coming from places as diverse as Regina and Halifax) but that vital contact with a mass movement just beginning to feel its strength, to flex its muscles, was gone. I asked her if she felt the movement had let her down, leaving her in the "high" stranded in mid-air. "Good God, no. It's never let me down. If anything, I let it down. I should have been attending meetings, seeing if there was anything I could do. But I got away from it all for a while."

It was one thing, sitting in the tight circle of female guides, to locate your victimization. It was another thing, all on your own, facing bewildered husband and children, hostile relatives, and timorous housewife friends, to break out quickly and cleanly. Hence the procrastination, the wavering, the fearfulness. Maybe things aren't so bad after all? Maybe she wouldn't actually have to leave? Maybe in two months she would feel stronger? Where were her chances better of going off the deep end—here in this stupefying kitchen or out there by herself among the machinery of a woman-hating public? How, in other words, could you break the paralyzing tension between knowing you have been a victim and knowing too that you have the responsibility and the will to be otherwise?

Not that she doesn't know what she wants to do. Leave home, with or without both children. Get a better part-time job. Lose weight. Get back in touch with feminist groups. Retrain her voice. Cut an album. Organize a home for runaway mothers. Help in the anti-abortion law campaign. Set up a Women's Liberation School or summer camp.

She's talked about it with David. He says he knows she literally can't live without Women's Liberation; he's listened to her reports from all the Caucus meetings, he's heard her music, he's looked through her *Ms* magazines that she laid out for him one night, here look at this and this, you see what I mean? He said if he was a woman he wouldn't want to live like that, either. She should get out and fight for herself. Sure, he's afraid she may not come back but he's willing to take the chance. For that matter, she's scared, too. She walks out the door and maybe her world falls apart. She's just too damn chicken. Hell, it's falling apart anyway. "I want it and then I don't want it and then I do again. I'm so mixed-up, inconsistent. But, oh God, it sounds exciting, so good!" I tell her about a friend of mine who said that leaving home is good for your mental health. We laugh.

> "Tell it like it is, sisters, tell it like it is.
> Tell it like it is, sisters, tell it like it is.
> Control of our bodies, control of our minds.
> Control of our bodies, control of our lives."

The three of us are sitting around the kitchen table, Rita, her friend and myself. We're really enjoying the conversation. For once, I'm as active as my interviewees. That's a good feeling, to return the favour of exposure by opening yourself up, too. But in the end they really do the talking. After all, they're the ones who have children, cook three meals a day and iron shirts, and this is what I came to find out about.

The conversation skips around. A coalminer's life in Cape Breton. A TV show about rape. How children don't necessarily ruin your life but do determine where it's going to go (you can't just pick up and leave . . .). Rita's recent therapeutic abortion and tubal ligation and the big scene at the hospital when it was discovered that David hadn't signed the papers for the operations. Fears about contraceptive methods, women used as guinea pigs for male researchers, the side-effects of the pill. Rita's rejection of Catholicism when, suddenly, the teachings about "my woman's duty and God's will just didn't sink in any more." The burning of Joan of Arc and the so-called witches. Marriage and the death of the personality, the loss of courage and the failure of intelligence. The hateful household routine, especially, for Rita, the cooking. "I *hate* having to get a meal ready every single day at five o'clock. David says he likes me because I'm not dull. When he comes home from work he doesn't know what to expect: supper on the table or a plate fired at the door, *I'm not cooking*!" How awful we think our bodies are. How housewives get into booze and pills. An offensive, sexist cigarette ad. "Girltalk". These conversations are our lifejackets which keep us afloat above the bullshit. Exercises in sanity. Offerings at the gynocratic confessional: "What I do realize now is that I'm a very strong feminist, stronger than I thought and I've been trying hard to live with a lot of things and I just can't do it any more. I'm just ready to . . . I'm going to move out. I'm going to fight."

When last I saw Rita, she had an exercise bicycle in her kitchen and her sister-in-law was supervising her diet. She had been downtown to check out a place to live. She had sung at York University, at a benefit for Women's Place and had just recorded the last cut on a tape that may become an album. An illustrated book of her songs was about to be published. She is, in the end, a singer.

The experience in the recording studio, with an unexpectedly sensitive and unpretentious arranger/producer, with a group of musicians genuinely interested in her music and what she is trying to say, was "overwhelming, I've never experienced anything like it. It was very hard at times, very emotional, trying to get through some of the songs. I'm sure other people going into that studio would have got it right the first time. Maybe I'm *too* emotional. I just feel it all too much. Every time I sing, 'Who Will I Go To See?' I crack up. It's a raw thing, you just cut yourself open. But I don't know any other way to be. I just can't hold back. And I just don't know if that's good for me any more." So maybe this studio trip, her voice breaking in tears at times, the guitar and violins filling in the simple, lovely melodies she had first hummed late at night to herself, too excited to sleep, was a purge of sorts. She's expelled the heaviest things that have been a long time on her mind, now it's time to live differently.

Even her mother's last, admonishing letter to her isn't going to change her mind: "You should be a gospel singer or a Western (one). I don't think you'll get anywhere with this Women's Lib." But Rita, although she lovingly keeps this letter close at hand, has refused her mother's destiny. She's re-appropriating her life, getting back what's hers from all the people and places where she had distributed herself. She's going to survive. Her music is both the talisman that sees her through, and the booty at the end of the trip. She calls it "little feelings". She is too modest. They're big feelings and a hopeful politics. "If only," a friend has said, "she knew how badly we need to hear her."

Esther Warkov:
Painting for God and Wall Street

BY MELINDA McCRACKEN

The old pawnshops and cafes of Main Street in Winnipeg's North End near the Salter Street Bridge are a ramshackle record of prairie growth—grain, railroading, immigration, and hard times. While much of the rest of residential Winnipeg is suburban and Anglo-Saxon, the North End has always been ethnic—Jews, Ukrainians, Poles, Germans, Swedes, Indians, and Métis. Most of the buildings are old frame houses of various shapes and sizes jumbled together with small stores on the corner, and the heterogeneous character of the neighbourhood is apparent in the variety of houses.

Still, just before the suburb of West Kildonan, you can find streets of prosperous-looking square white postwar houses, similar to those in upper-middle-class River Heights, where the successful sons and daughters of first-generation ethnics live. With fir trees in the front yards and cedar trees at the side, these manicured dwellings have bouquets of flowers displayed in the picture window, sidewalks shoveled to the brown cement through the Dream Whip snow, and the aluminum snow shovel left casually by the front door, a promise to the neighbours that Standards Will Be Met. Behind or attached are matching white stucco garages, which shelter cars that transport these comfortable cushioned lives through the snow to Eaton's, Loblaw's, and to work and back.

The houses look polished, as if time is spent caring for them and the lives within. Life within the houses appears to be lived for life, and not sacrificed for anything else. The houses send out messages of reassurance to the neighbours that yes, we have our wall-to-wall carpet tacked to the living room floor, yes, our chesterfield is flanked by matching end tables just like yours. Nor have we broken faith and removed the cellophane from the white silk shades of our matching table lamps, and our dining room suite stands tidily in the dining room under the chandelier, and likewise the bedroom suite in the bedroom. And we eat and sleep and bring up our children and go to work and keep the house clean and cared for, just as you do, and time passes and the children grow and we grow older and more prosperous, and, yes, we are fairly happy, like you.

But there is something about one of these houses—a two-storey white stucco box, with a picture window, cement front steps, and the family initial in the aluminum front door—that is not reassuring at all, that is positively disturbing. There is nothing comfortable or cushioned about it. The front walk isn't shoveled. There are no floral arrangements set on polished dropleaf tables in the picture windows. The white paint and green trim are a little weatherbeaten; the house appears lean, hollow, baring its unpadded bones to the elements, and it seems to be trying to push itself up into the prairie sky.

The impression is no illusion. Inside, instead of the predictable middle-class shine and softness that are implicit in the house's straight boxy lines, the rooms are practically empty. The gold flocked wallpaper is there in the dining room, of course, and so are the small crystal chandeliers. But the trappings of a solid middle-class lifestyle stop right there. For where the dining room suite should be stand two beds. The gold broadloom is beat-up and spotty, and the plaster walls are bare and smudged. In the living room stands an old dentist's chair, such as might be the prized possession of a hippy commune. In the window, in a wooden cage, are two fawn-coloured doves that coo softly, purringly. There is a large pile of expensive-looking coffee-table picture books, but no coffee table. Things stand around the edges of the rooms—weeds, shells, stones, a stuffed falcon, a bright blue director's chair, a couple of black bentwood chairs, an ornate old mantle clock—as if they've been brought in for a while to see how they do, and could be rejected the moment they lose favour. The objects are elegant and interesting; if an effort were made to decorate the rooms according to the inhabitants' taste, the result might be quite wonderful, but there's no time for that. The halls are full of canvases in transit upstairs to a studio or to another out in the garage. The kitchen is bare and empty, without much association with food. There are no daisies on the walls, or avocado-coloured appliances or evidence of any sunny scenes with kids praising the quality of today's Sugar Pops around the breakfast table. Rather, it looks as if every meal here is an eat-and-run affair.

The clash between the middle-class structure and the atmosphere in the house is unsettling. To a visitor, it is strange enough to be threatening. The doves coo ominously, the falcon seems to be pouncing on its prey; you almost expect a Venus flytrap to reach out and clamp you on the elbow as you're passing through.

Behind the house a narrow grey path beaten past a couple of garden chairs submerged in the snow leads out to the white stucco garage. The sun on the snow outside the garage is dazzling, but inside, the light from two fluorescent tubes is a disappointing greyish white. There are no cars in the garage, no power tools or husbandly workshop, no transparent green plastic coils of garden hose or aluminum garden chairs with woven plastic seats, no barbecue briquets or half-empty cans of Charco-Lite waiting for the return of summer, no signs that that sort of life goes on at all. The floor of the garage is sticky with spilled paint and masking tape. More books and magazines full of pictures lie about, one a book on the American hand-gun containing black and white photographs of potbellied sharpshooters pulling revolvers from their holsters, another a 1927 Sears, Rocbuck catalogue, beside a metal music stand upon which the books can be clipped open. Scraps of aluminum foil with patches of brownish and orangish and pinkish paint on them are spread over a work table and stuck to the wall. By the small door at the front is an antique hat rack with an oval mirror in the back, and at the far end of the garage, by the green overhead doors, in a jumble of canvases, stretchers, and paintings, sits an unmade rollaway cot.

But spread out on stands in all their glory, dominating the whole garage, is a panorama of paintings on several canvases of various sizes, which make up a total of two paintings. On the large square canvas on the left is the three-quarter profile of a man wearing a fedora, a shapely *Sting*-style hat from the Sears, Roebuck catalogue. The man's face, in warm brown tones, is alive with flowers and insects and is made to stand out sharply, like a flat cutout, at the front of the canvas by a salmon coloured background. On another large canvas a man with wings on his back sits at a table, and on the largest canvas closest to the door, the brown figure of a Botticelli Venus, cut off at the feet, rises up from the edge of the canvas, bees coming out of her hands, and beside her, the swirling stem of a large brown rose, its head teeming with life—flowers, bugs, traceries, and the man in the fedora only smaller this time, set against an empty expanding blue that causes the brown shapes to converge in upon themselves. Clouds dot the sky and by Venus's legs, tile-like squares fade back into the blue.

The paintings are very powerful; they seem to diminish people looking at them, not by their size, which is considerable, but by the serenity of the resolution of their elements, as if they serve to condense a higher reality onto the material plane. Their muted colours are beautiful, especially against the cell-like drabness of the garage.

The small figure in paint-spattered jeans standing by the paintings like a proud landlady showing her property is the artist, Esther Warkov. She is very small, five-feet-two, much smaller than the paintings, and standing there, she doesn't draw herself up to her full height like the caterpillar in *Alice in Wonderland*, but slouches like a hippy, as if to say height has nothing on her. Her hair is short and dark brown, her features fine, and her mouth curves in a sly grin that's as ready to put you on as it is to be friendly, depending on how you turn out.

Her voice is flat and urban, the voice of a young Jewish society woman. She seems to know that's what it sounds like, and plays on the cliché, parodying it with conscious use of expressions like "You know what it's like", delivered in a flat, world-weary tone. She rolls her words in a childish way and often conducts the timing of the conversation like a comedienne:

"This year I didn't get a Canada Council Grant, but my gallery is supporting me. When the guy at the Council writes you a letter he calls you 'Madame'. I think maybe I should turn into a high-priced prostitute—though inflation has been going up and my measurements have stayed the same. I think of my cleavage as a dead-end street between two empty parking lots.

"Someone said that talking to me is like going through a revolving door," she says. "I just rush around things a little too much." It's true; she does tend to let her thoughts run away with her, and also, curiously, she forgets her train of thought just at the point when the listener's attention flags. Her conversation is rich and playful and full of switchbacks, yet not particularly lucid, as if talking is something she associates with entertainment, and not with self expression. When she says "today"—"Then you begin to think like a sociologist, you know, *today* what it's like," you wonder if she really knows what's going on in the outside world today, or if like a hermit or Rip Van Winkle, she just *thinks* that's what's going on, out there—and furthermore you wonder if she really cares. Because she's been in the garage for 14 years. "It's not very attractive, is it," she says, looking around good-naturedly at the mess.

"You expect to see a lot of potted plants and draperies, and it's a big dump." She says they feed her through the window now.

By beating the grey trail through the snow out to her garage every day for the past 14 years, Esther Warkov has become one of the best artists in Canada. Her paintings are sold by the Marlborough Godard Gallery, an international gallery and one of the world's largest, with branches in Switzerland, Italy, England, Japan, New York, and Montreal and Toronto. The price of one of her paintings may be about four thousand dollars. She has had six individual shows and will have a seventh in May of 1975 in Montreal, and has participated in about fifteen group exhibitions, including one last fall of the gallery's artists in New York. Her paintings hang in galleries and private collections all over the U.S. and Canada. To achieve this, she has lived on four Canada Council bursaries and one major grant, and the income from her paintings.

She does nothing but paint. To say that her social life is restricted would be an understatement, like her own dry comment, "I don't hold little dinner parties". In fact as a social being she ranks with a hermit. When I asked her about her friends in Winnipeg, she said quite simply that, apart from her husband, she had no friends in Winnipeg—and that is despite the fact that she has lived her entire life there. Her life outside the house revolves around her work—she only goes downtown for necessities, she only travels to take pictures for her work, and her only grand social events are openings of exhibitions which she attends quietly, making no effort to draw attention to her work. Life for her revolves around the latest canvas in the garage.

Out in her garage in 40 below weather, she works in warm clothes, melton cloth ski pants stuffed into the tops of rubber combat boots. When she's drawing she sits at a table piled high with coffee-table books, beside a large supply of blue Mars Lumigraph pencils with leads of varying hardnesses, like a captain at the Wheel of her ship, looking up occasionally to watch "The Edge of Night" flicker on the small black and white TV across the room. Watching "The Edge of Night", the traditional pastime of housewives bored out of their minds, is not a fetish unique to her. P.G. Wodehouse, the Edwardian humorist who died only recently, was another unlikely devotee of the TV soap opera.

Anyone who can stay there permanently in the garage, who can force herself to sit there all the time, bringing paintings and drawings, one after another, to a long and laborious realization—while at the same time being a mother, a wife, and attending to her own human needs such as eating and sleeping—anyone who can do this is clearly a very strong person, a self-reliant loner. And when you are with Esther you are aware that you are in the presence of someone special. There, lurking behind her facade of black humour, is someone who seems to be able to see right through you. And when you look up accidentally to find yourself fixed by large black eyes shimmering with something a little wild and uncanny, the atmosphere is scary. Yet in no way does she stifle you or put you down; provided you are honest with her, she is supportive, open, and generous.

Warkov's work has reflected many influences—surrealists like de Chirico, primitives like Henri Rousseau, medieval and traditional masters, and practitioners of American pop art. But her work changes all the time. She paints to last. Her technique is slow and painstaking, like that of the old masters. A major portion of her time is spent preparing her canvas.

"First, my canvas is stretched," she says, "and I put one coat of rabbit-skin glue on it. Then I put five coats of gesso, with sandings in between each coat that take 15 or 10 minutes each. The first sanding takes an hour. And then I put on three coats of acrylic, and then I put one coat of oil paint on that. Then I might paint a butterfly and then I repaint the butterfly again, and then I put the details, repaint details, put other details on top of them, et cetera, et cetera. It's a pain in the ass."

Clearly, though, she thinks the pain in the ass is worth it. "I guess it's sort of old-fashioned, but I paint for myself and art history. I really want to be up there with the biggies, I really want to be thought of as a good artist. I want to say something and say it well, even if it isn't a great deal." But unlike abstract expressionists, it's not the *process* of painting that matters to her. The most important part is the result, "the end image, how it works and clicks and looks good visually".

Most of her paintings are on several rectangular and circular canvases, sometimes five or more, hinged together, or with a separate circular canvas hanging nearby; using more than a single rectangular canvas gives her compositional sense more scope. The foundation of the painting is a classically ordered resolution. Her compositions are predominantly horizontal and vertical, with few diagonal or oblique lines. Often her images are right up at the front of the canvas, with spaces and ovals and doors looking through to infinite space beyond.

Since her first concern is visual impact, images are used first because they fit the composition; no literal meaning is intended by the fact that certain images—perhaps conflicting ones—have been put in the same painting. There is usually a human being in every painting; because she finds people hard to draw, Esther says she feels she's cheated herself unless she puts a person in each painting. Usually the person in the painting is doing something quite familiar. The woman having her hair combed out by a hairdresser in "Madonna of the Golden Pears" was taken from a photograph of Esther's mother at the beauty salon. The man sitting reading a newspaper in "Memories of an Autumn Day" is from a photograph of her father.

Often she puts things together that simply don't go together in the ordinary world. A man sits in a restaurant booth eating daisies off a plate, while a Henri Rousseau-like lion stalks the air behind him. A black man with white wings ascends into the air after crucifixion. A truck carries a load of nudes. Things turn into other things—a motorcycle carburetor becomes a man, a woman a butterfly, a spark plug becomes a winged victory. As well, her paintings are strewn with elements of past styles, Victorian and Thirties style clothing, old furniture, people with beards in starched collars, old bridal gowns, New England white frame churches. And over and around the images are strewn flowers and insects and details in tracery, like a blessing. "Visually, I'm more innocent than a lot of artists," she says. "Like, I think wedding dresses are beautiful, and I know I'm not supposed to think that because I'm liberated. I mean, I really believe in women's lib, but at the same time I think wedding gowns are beautiful. I imagine myself getting married in a railway yard, in a wedding gown, with angels. I love flowers and I love children and all this—and at the same time I'm supposed to be liberated."

The things she puts in her paintings appear to be chosen simply because she thinks they are beautiful. But although people constantly try to read a meaning into her work, she doesn't feel the images in her paintings are symbolic. "A lot of people say my work is very literary. They think it's symbolic. Like, they say, what does this mean, and I say, that's a flower. I really am very visual."

There is little of the prairies in Esther's work. Despite her Winnipeg background she identifies with the east, and since her experience is not small town Manitoba, nor Protestant, she doesn't think of herself as a prairie person. "I do have farmers in my work, but they're not really milking cows and doing all those other things. My background is really urban." Many of the pictures she uses in her work are from American books, and her influence is more North American than specifically Canadian. "I've never had this hate-love relationship with Canada, and I've never left Canada and condemned it, which I know some artists have done. I've survived all those people, and I think in some cases they've resented me because I've stayed here, seemed to be quite happy and done my work."

Her opinions on other artists are competitively cheeky. "Alexander Colville, I call him Coldville, I don't like him too much. And there's Christopher Pratt, I call him Christopher Drab. They're not really realists, photographic realists. Pratt's a better painter than Colville, although I think Colville has more to say; but all that cross hatching—it's so blah! And the Group of Seven: I don't care for that whole school, I think it's junk. It's just not visually very interesting. It had some value in terms of the myths it's built up about the people, but as art, a lot of it is really very second rate. I know what they were trying to say, but I think people have talked them up a lot. I think when you take the paintings away from the talk, you see they were nice little landscapes. You know, with a tree here, a little river. And it *is* sort of romantic, the idea of sitting out there in the middle of winter freezing your ass off, painting nature."

In the same admittedly arrogant vein she referred to a current exhibition at the Winnipeg Art Gallery called "Cosmic Variations" as Cosmic Crap. "When you get down to it, it's just circles on a page. And you can say that about my work, that I do bugs and people turning into bugs and things growing out of things, machines becoming people, et cetera. So whenever someone asks me what I do, I say, well, that's a girl in the corner and that's a blue colour. I just like to put things together and see how they come out."

Esther Warkov was born in the northern part of the North End, closer to Selkirk Avenue, and moved to the same house she lives in now when she was 9. While she was growing up, she went to the parochial school, called the Talmud Torah, until grade 8. It was Zionist and Hebrew orientated, as opposed to the Peretz school, which was more European. They offered Yiddish literature and stories by authors like Sholem Aleichem and she learned to read in Hebrew "at 60 miles an hour", but didn't understand what she was reading. "They never talked about their own artists," she says, "and didn't concentrate on the creative aspects." So Esther received no exposure to art there. She went to St. John's Tech. for high school and failed grade 11. She took tutoring in math in grade 11 from a man who made jewellery, and liked the art more than the maths, so instead of writing supps, took a summer course in art. It wasn't until she went into first year fine art at the University of Manitoba School of Art, that she found out who Chagall was.

At that point in her life, she felt like a failure. There were her parents, worried that she wasn't going to get married to the right Jewish boy. "None of the right people were asking me out. I just got the leftovers, you know, the ugly, the fat, and the dumb. But never the successes. And all of the good choices were taken up by the time you were about 18. In those days you got married quick, like to avoid becoming old at the age of twenty. So I had nothing to worry about. I went quietly on my own way."

"My parents didn't want me to continue in art school, so I had one professor write a letter to say that I was a really good artist. So he wrote and said that I had talent and that I should be allowed to be kept in school." Her parents didn't approve of her ambition. "I tried to sell my clothes to buy paint, because I wasn't selling any of my work, which wasn't worth buying anyways, and it was expensive to buy material at the time. So I threatened that if my parents didn't let me stay in school, I'd burn the house down. Little things like that. I'm kind of dedicated."

Life and her parents' expectations went one way, and Esther went another. The boys she went out with were boys she met at the art school, people who had very little money and didn't have enough to eat. "I used to steal food from my house. I would steal oranges and apples and things and sandwiches from the house and carry them out. But I think my parents knew what I was doing, because I was always walking off with these big bags."

At art school, she started off in sculpture and was very pleased. But the new sculpture teacher didn't like her, so she didn't go back the next year, going into painting instead. "I never had any talent when I began. I could never draw. And all the other people would be drawing hands in 25 different positions with their eyes closed, and I was always struggling. I had to teach myself everything. Not that I've learnt everything, but I had to teach myself how to do it. I didn't have any natural ability, let's put it that way. And I didn't know anything about art. I had never been to an art exhibit or anything like that. The professors in the art school were artists who were using the school to make a living while they painted, and sometimes they didn't ever show up for class. They didn't teach the students any rigorous classical drawing or even basic things like how to stretch canvas or build stretchers."

The only way to survive in the school situation was to go ahead and work on your own, which she did. She started looking at the books they had there, and then would copy from them. She copied everything she could find—The Fauves, the Impressionists, Van Gogh, everyone she saw. It was discouraging, she says, because she wasn't a very good copier. But she was able to teach herself the technical things the teachers overlooked, and through the exposure to books and to people around her making art, she learned quite a bit. Then in third year, without staying around for her degree, she moved into the garage and kept on painting. She met her husband in art school, and they were married in 1966, and in 1969 Jenny arrived. Usually the arrival of a child imposes terrible strains on a woman involved in her career. But when Jenny was small, Esther's husband, who is also a painter and works in the studio upstairs, took care of her in the afternoons while Esther painted, and she took care of her in the mornings while he painted. Now Jenny, a slender, fine-featured, blonde five-year-old, very quick, with spaces between her small even teeth, goes to nursery school in the afternoons.

Even though Esther is a successful artist, she still has to struggle. The most she can produce in a year is seven paintings and about 30 drawings. "I figure this year, I have maybe eighteen thousand dollars worth of stuff, and the gallery, like most galleries, takes a 40 per cent commission to offset the expenses of running a gallery. So you know what that leaves me with—with nothing. If you sell everything it's not the case. It looks like I'm successful, but I'm not in a way, because I'm just sort of living on the good graces of people. The expense of being a visual artist, the space you need, you have to build crates, you have to have people make your stretchers, maybe I spend over twelve hundred a year on supplies. It's a continuous struggle just to keep going.

As a woman has she encountered prejudice in the art world? "I think as a man, I'd have gotten farther than I have today. I have that feeling. There are other male figurative artists whom I'm as good as, and better, who've had almost whole issues of *artscanada* devoted to their art. And I have not, just the occasional short review. I'm sort of on the periphery." It's partly due to the fact that so much attention has been paid to hard-edge and colour-field painting, and partly due to the fact that she has let her work stand on its own without calling attention to it. "I'm much too arrogant for that," she says.

She goes diligently out to her garage every day. "I think about my art fairly often," she says, meaning all the time, "and I think, well, I've got to go out there and do my flowers and it's 45 below. I work all the time." She does go outside; she goes from the house to the garage and from the garage to the house, and sometimes she goes downtown, so she does see other things besides the garage. "It can be depressing at times. I have to force myself to work. And you get a closed-in feeling after a while. I don't mind it in here, though, really, because I have my work. I try to work, not every day, but five days a week, because I have to keep doing it, otherwise I wouldn't get anything done. As it is, I could do more paintings. It seems I've always done about the same amount of work, it's just that I can do it quicker now."

Working all the time creates other problems. "I get panicky. Every morning when I get up, I get panicky. Always saying, look, gotta go into the studio, gotta work. Because in a sense I think some artists would feel that the only good thing about them is their work. This gives them an identity. And take that away, and no one will talk to you or be your friend. You know, where you place so much emphasis on what you do, and it drives you to do more, you don't necessarily enjoy it while you're doing it. It's only when I almost reach the end of a painting when I begin to enjoy what I'm doing. And then I feel that if each painting that I do is not a success, then I'm a failure as an artist, which is not a good attitude to have. You know, you get very anxious.

"It's a lonely life. There's nobody coming around and saying that's beautiful, that's wonderful. And then you do your work and you might have terrible reviews. Which I've had. That doesn't bother me. It did when I was younger, but now that I'm older that doesn't bother me, because I'm more secure and self-confident in my lack of talent."

Why does she paint? "That's the only thing I'm good at," she says. "I sort of paint for God and Wall Street, I've got them both. I don't have a lot of hobbies. And I'm sort of underwhelmed by life. I'm kind of quiet. And I don't think I have a lot of energy for a lot of other things. I do one thing, and I do it rather well, and that satisfies me.".

Her life undoubtedly would not satisfy most people. Watching the "Edge of Night" is not associated with uplifting work, but at least she, unlike other housewives, has something to do with her hands while she watches TV in the afternoons. Her life is one of permanent commitment to her work, and she is so entrenched in it, she almost seems part of the house. Except for shows and grants, there are almost no events in her life.

Dedicating one's life to one's art is a profound commitment, but Esther doesn't seem to have suffered from it. Her face is clear and youthful. And her acceptance of her life situation is enviable. "I'll always live in this house," she says. "I'll always be a painter." If all goes well, both God and Wall Street will be impressed.

Portrait of Barbara

BY ERNA PARIS

I always see her in colours—red, orange, coral, sometimes brown. She says she was black for several years. Sometimes she's quite wild, like a gypsy, blowing in and out and all over the place. She also likes to get drunk, and when she does she's got a laugh to shake down a house. So could her sobs, for that matter, if that's the way her mood shifts.

Barbara Greene is my friend. She's made some bad moves and suffered disappointment like everyone else, but I think she's a great woman. I love her joy and her energy and the way she reflects these feelings in her work in radio and film. I admire her willingness to remain vulnerable though she's 50 now, and the way she has had the courage to look honestly at herself and become independent. Sometimes she falls on her face, but Barbara's taken chances on things that would scare the bejesus out of some people—especially those who seal wax over the tops of their lives and think they are safe.

If you're a downtown habitué of Toronto or Montreal you may see her one day. Barbara is about 5′ 4″ and she's full look-ing and sort of sloppy. Her hair used to be blonde, but it's grey now, and messy-wispy around her face. If it's cool, she may be wearing a broad-brimmed red felt hat, a suede vest that's faded to a nondescript grey-beige, with brass dome fasteners down the middle, baggy, style-defying pants, and a black cape. If the weather is warm she'll probably appear in a long dress made of rough, natural white cotton that makes her look like a Wagnerian soprano, or else a mini that's too short for anyone

151

who doesn't have stick legs, but suits her just fine because it keeps the air circulating.

The lines are running deep around her mouth and eyes now, but her eyes are very blue, and they usually look as though they've just seen something funny. Sometimes it's hard to anticipate whether they will shoot out sparks of humour, accompanied by the percussion of an enormous belly laugh, or whether they'll suddenly brim with easy tragedy. Barbara lives on the sharp edge of emotion, ready to fall either way.

She calls these her "big feelings", great reserves of energy ready to explode into screeching laughter, tears, dance, strong yearnings, or concentrated work. Her hunger and her appetites push her on; she gobbles experience with intense, voracious pleasure. Barbara has always been hungry, quite literally. Invite her for dinner and she'll smack her lips if it's good or lick her fingers greedily. In conversation, she hugs and paws people in her enthusiasm, and is looked upon as unseemly by the genteel and the pompous. But children, who are not to be fooled, recognize her spirit. "Can Barbara come out to play?" asked a small person one day when I answered the door of her home.

Barbara has spent a lot of time shedding old skins that have become too tight, and bravely trying on new ones for size. She may tell you she doesn't feel like a success story, that she has too many conflicts and feels too much loneliness for that. But what she has achieved is truly remarkable. Barbara has stripped down to her naked life force and you can practically *see* the darn thing fill her up and lift her off the ground like a helium balloon. Even when she's miserable, hers is no mean, poking sadness. It's as monumental as her laughter. Both her sadness and her joy embrace her and all the spaces around.

In 1923, when she was born, the village of Quathiaski Cove on Quadra Island, one hundred miles north of Vancouver, seemed like the edge of the world. From her parents' home on the hill she could look over the towering Douglas firs to the sea and the thin line of the horizon drawn along its furthest edge. The horizon was magic. Her father was magic, too. He was a Church of England missionary, and he would sail over the world's edge, in his boat, *The Rendezvous*, to visit his parishioners in the tiny settlements up and down the coast. He also had a portable organ that he'd named "Little Jimmy" and he'd take it ashore with him and play hymns. Every couple of weeks he'd return, his eyes shining, full of marvellous stories about the lives of the people he had seen. Barbara loved him and she yearned to be his companion on the boat. When she was very little she'd lie in bed listening to the fog horns and wonder where he was on the magic sea.

Boys, it seemed to her then, could do just about anything they liked. They could wear jeans, work in the cannery, go out on the boats alone, play any game they wanted, be rough, and fight—and they were *expected* to climb trees. The sea was a place of wandering and exploration but was accessible only to them. "I dreamt of myself in a sailor suit standing at the helm of my father's boat, but as a girl child it all seemed impossible."

Experience lay over the sea, past Quathiaski Cove with its 100 inhabitants. When she grew up she would *move*, just like her father. Push off from the shore and keep going.

And so she has. Barbara is first and foremost a wanderer in pursuit of experience. Her I.D. card is a tape recorder; that pass-key to other people's lives that allows her to ask a lot of personal questions which are really none of her business. She has a vital combination of boldness and sensitivity that allows her to reach that gut centre where a person's truth lies, and to coax something real to the surface, without offending. And like every good interviewer, she's incurably nosy.

She was quick to develop her taste for whatever is strange and off-beat. In Quathiaski Cove the settlers were often people who hadn't made it elsewhere, and some of them were odd in ways fascinating to a child. Every few days Mr. Pichee "appeared" from around the point, in his dugout rowboat, to buy his groceries at the general store on the wharf. He always wore many hats and he'd amaze the children by removing them, one by one, like tightly-nested Russian dolls. And then there was Twothumbs, a Chinese who really had two thumbs on his left hand and who scared the children by poking his thumbs in their faces. And old Louise, who wheedled the storekeeper into selling her bottles of vanilla extract so she could "bake cakes". On Quadra people sometimes drank for recreation, and on Friday evenings Barbara would stand at the top of the hill and watch them disappear in their boats across to the Willow Hotel beer parlour at Campbell River. She was deeply curious and excited by this mysterious activity and by the raucous behaviour of the returning boatloads. Particularly since there was no alcohol in the minister's home.

Being the minister's daughter wasn't easy. God was embarrassing. He made Barbara and her brothers and sisters feel different from everybody else—hell, it was no fun having the village church in their very backyard. Later, in church, while everyone sang the response, "Lord, incline our hearts to keep this law," Barbara sang as loud as she dared, "Lord, incline our hearts to *break* this law."

"I had all the makings of a rebellious person and an oddball," she says, "though as a child I often hid these feelings. Inside I worried about what was expected of me as a girl; I felt disturbed about being feminine and what it was supposed to mean."

Femininity was confusing because her mother, whom she loved, was very feminine, very selfless, and often very sad. She kept the house happy and cheerful for the children. She cooked, and washed, and ironed, and mended, and welcomed her children's friends into her home. She was deeply involved in the lives of the people in the settlement. She ran the village Sunday School and encouraged the teacher in the one-room school house with her music program. When her husband returned from sea she welcomed him lovingly, and she wrote faithfully and regularly to her family in "the East". The return letters were read formally to her children seated around the dining room table, so that they wouldn't lose touch with their relatives. She was very beautiful. And sometimes she cried at night.

Barbara's mother had come to the bush in 1919 from the carefully-manicured, tree-lined streets of Rosedale, the "best" district in Toronto. And, as in the case of that other gently reared lady, Susanna Moodie, the uprooting was difficult, and the transplant never really took. She had been educated to be a lady, first at Havergal College, a private school for the daughters of the rich, and later at a finishing school where she had learned Old English script writing, drawing, and sketching. As a young woman she sang in the church choir and everyone said that she had a fine voice. Barbara's father was a theology student at the University of Toronto—a jolly, life-hugging, irresistibly attractive man—and their first home was a boat off the coast. There she became both seasick and pregnant, but she still wrote cheerfully to Toronto describing what her new life would be once they landed and the baby was born. The children came every two years, six of them, though one died.

Barbara's mother was a deeply religious woman who believed that a woman's appointed role was to join forces with a man and help him in his work. When she needed strength, as she so often did, she prayed. It was a lonely life with her husband gone most of the time, although when he came home, he was attentive to her and the children; but Barbara, for one, thought jealously that there were many women up and down the coast who saw her father as often as her mother did, and many children, too, who were bounced on his knees with the same enthusiasm.

She had a piano shipped into Quathiaski Cove with the music she had played and sung as a girl, and for over thirty years she played "Cherry Ripe", "Danny Boy", "Oh Promise

Me", never updating her repertoire, the point being not the music but what she had left behind. But evenings were the time Barbara felt her mother's sadness most. After the children were put to bed she would play hymns until she thought they were asleep and then she would go to the kitchen to iron. "Sometimes I would hear her cry and wonder what she was thinking about and where my father was at that moment. Then I'd leave my bed and sit on a stool beside her in the kitchen, silently. I'd feel some terrible weariness in her—as though all her energy were streaming down through her arm into the iron."

Femininity, or a woman's life as Barbara saw her mother live it, seemed deeply unsatisfying. "Mother didn't ask enough for herself. She was a vital woman and active in the community, but she had a saintlike quality that was hard for me to live with. She put everyone else ahead of herself. Some of my own sadness at times comes from the fact that my needs, and my passions, were not recognized. A child is a piggy monster and if your mother is trying to help you be selfless and you want your way, badly, it's hard. I have had to learn on my own that it is not immoral to put myself first and to respect my own creativity and needs. To give and give and give and never take is stifling. How can a child take on God? Where does all the energy go?"

When Barbara was 14 the family moved to Vancouver. Leaving the rough edges of the woods for cement and planted gardens and a school with 1500 students terrified her after the single room in Quathiaski Cove. "I felt like a perfect hick. I didn't understand the middle-class neighbourhood and all the houses that looked so much alike, and the notion of standard economic security." But by the time she reached UBC she had emerged as a student leader, "larger than life". Personal problems were emerging. "I kept trying so hard, but I never got close to anyone. And I began to develop a sort of double consciousness that persisted until I got therapy several years later. It was a sense of the distance between the person I *appeared* to be and what I really felt. On the outside I was popular, active, funny, fun-loving—and I smiled. God, I smiled all the time, but inside I still didn't know how to express my energies, and I felt very alone."

Somehow, Barbara never got married when all her friends did. For one thing she was still focused on a life of exploration and travel. And then, she distanced herself from other people—in the same way she created a "double-consciousness" within herself. "It wasn't that I consciously wanted distance, but I was afraid to take the risk of becoming dependent on someone. When you're vulnerable you risk getting hurt— someone you decide to love might leave you. I also looked like an independent woman, and that scared a lot of people."

Her twenties were difficult years, she says, but they were also the years when she began to make the important decisions that have shaped her life. After graduation in 1945 she decided to begin the travels she had dreamed of as a child staring at the sea. Her romantic visions of travel had also been nourished by a school collection called *Highroads to History*. They were books to stir the imagination, with vivid colour illustrations of the kings and queens of England and the history of the British Isles. Set against the cultural barrenness of Quadra Island, England looked rich, complex, and fascinating. Europe would be the destination, she thought, when she was ready. "I was afraid to go too soon, thinking I might hurt myself in some way. But even when I was little I would tell my mother I was going, and she would look at me as if I were mad."

In 1945 Barbara still wasn't "ready" for Europe, but Canada would do for a start. No one hitch-hiked then. There weren't many cars and even less gas, and the very *thought* of women on the road raised prickles up and down the backbones of respectable people. But Barbara was going to travel and get her experience first hand. She went off with a hardy girlfriend and they stood along the side of the highway surrounded by family and well-wishers until a car picked them up and the wanderings began.

"When my mother saw us leave she wept and whispered in my ear, 'I think it's wonderful. I wish I were going with you.' "

The first voyage ended in Toronto, somewhat short of the Atlantic, and there Barbara became a social worker. It seemed closest to her instincts. What else would a minister's daughter do? Do good to others, be a responsible member of the community, "I'd been kind of an evil child distorting prayers in church and breaking the commandments all over the place. I had a sack of guilt to get rid of, and social work was, hmmm, comfortable.

"At home there had been a book called *Little Christian's Pilgrimage*, a child's version of *Pilgrim's Progress*. Little Christian went through many terrible things in order to get to the Celestial City, falling into the Slough of Despond and being rescued by the skin of his teeth—God it was terrible and absurd. During my social work years, I was still doing my pilgrimage, trying to be free of my parents and win their approval at the same time."

Social work was serious and demanding, working at first with a gang of tough kids struggling with their lives. But doubts began to come early. "I admired their strength in handling a messy situation, no home base and little attention, and their humour and their allegiance to each other. But I had been taught to be a 'professional' and outside their situation. I respected them, but I realized I wasn't deeply involved. Soon I would leave them. These temporary relationships provided them with a moment of warmth and love and fun—but they did nothing to change the system from which they'd come or the community where they lived, and that bothered me deeply." Later, there was the experience of working in a community centre in a working-class area and realizing that they didn't *want* a middle-class person mucking around with their lives. "They'd get drunk and say, 'Get the hell out, you don't belong.' I was playing a role in their lives the way my father played a professionally helpful role." She organized a cooperative day nursery, training the people themselves to take over—a generation ahead of the recent "power to the people" disciples—but some of her innovativeness caused conflict between her and other members of her profession. They said that she was "hostile to social work".

Personal relationships with men were less focused and less honest, at least in the early days. There was a boyfriend—a lot of boyfriends, in fact—but Barbara didn't sleep with them. She was still too close to the godliness of her parents' home. "You're limited and dishonest," said the boyfriend who was a liberated man at the age of twenty-two. "You fool around and tease. I don't want to see you again, but the next time you get together with a guy you'd better sleep with him or stop coming on strong." Barbara took his message seriously and went to bed with his best friend.

"You've taken something from me," said the best friend one night. "You aren't involved with me. I don't even know who you are. Why don't you ask your friends how many think of *you* as a friend?"

Barbara did, and the friends agreed that she was *not* their friend. She was devastated. She had thought that she was valued.

Between the laughing outside girl who worked capably at her job and enjoyed good times, and the remote and bloodless inner self a disturbing gulf was widening. Perceptive individuals, such as the man who had shared her bed, were beginning to see it and reject her. "I had to sort out this double lady I didn't understand. I was desperate; psychotherapy looked like an answer and it was. I was a pretty lady with pretty clothes. The analyst took them off and to my horror I had these strange ill-fitting rags underneath. I had to reassess who I was—I'd been hiding so long. It was difficult and painful, but in the end

I began to encounter myself as a whole being. I dropped the role of tease and flirt and began, tentatively, to live more honestly."

The first of the skins had been sloughed off.

From 1950 to 1954 Barbara concentrated on allowing the hidden and strange parts of herself to surface, exploding like bubbles long submerged in thick oil. As she reincorporated the pieces into a conscious whole, other areas of her life began to appear fragmented, like warped parts of a puzzle that no longer fit. Her work life and her play life, for instance. Social work was becoming less and less satisfying, ("Stupid," I'd say to myself, "where's *your* life in all of this?") and her night life had become more and more important. Evenings were when she did the things she *cared* about. She read, listened to music, partied with friends, painted, drank, laughed, and, now, slept with men. She began to believe that her life needn't be of two parts and that she was potentially a creative person.

Around age 30, all of this, and a lot of other changes were happening, too. She was feeling better physically, more energetic, powerful, ripe, and pleased to be a woman. Eventually she quit social work altogether. "I wanted to get on with my own self-exploration that I'd put off for so many years while I was doing the right thing by society. I also realized that the most effective way for me to operate was to use my whole personality, to show my face and all my rough edges and not hide inside a professional strait jacket. I knew that people had to see me and touch me as a real person in order to use my help, and that if I couldn't work that way, I couldn't stay in social work. Quitting completely was actually a relief. It was like dropping *Little Christian's Pilgrimage* and not atoning for all those 'sins' any more."

Another skin grown too tight and discarded. The decision, this time, was to leave Canada and take up the challenge of *Highroads to History*. Barbara took the $2000 she had saved and boarded ship. Eventually, she arrived in Spain and a little two-room house in Puerto de Andraitx, a Majorcan village.

The house in Majorca was small and simple, and, like all Barbara's environments, uncluttered and clear. She joined the landscape of international expatriates, drinking wine with them at noon in the Bar Central or later in the day with the fishermen, swimming, cooking beans or rice in her clay pots, and writing short stories based on the lives of the villagers. "I tried to go with the day. I learned that there was a lot I could do with my eyes, my hands, my mind, and my body. I had no clock and no appointments, nothing but the sea and the earth and the sky. I was being selfish and it was delicious and I slowly discovered the natural rhythms of my life. I decided then that I would never return to social work."

But there was still something missing, an intimacy, a closeness, sharing with a man. Barbara was still paying the original tithe of her independence, fearing to break the fragile thread of a life being carefully spun out length by length. Men were still to be enjoyed, of course, as honestly as possible. She was lonely, and she did not rule out the possibility of a sexual encounter. When travelling, the rules of the road were understood by all who passed. Mutual loneliness, mutual need. "Sometimes I'd decide to go to the theatre, for instance, or a concert of music I loved, and I'd wait until the lights were almost down before I chose a seat beside a man who was alone. It was very straightforward and honest."

What annoyed her most was that she was sometimes made to feel unnatural. "I needed and missed warmth. When you're not married you miss being in bed with someone, you miss someone's arms, you yearn to feel beautiful, worthwhile and acceptable. I also yearned for reassurance that I was a normal woman."

"I thought of myself as honest about sex but I was only a good lay to many of the men. That's all right. They were, too. But because I never lost sight of them as people—to me that was always most important—it was hurtful to be treated like a slut by men who didn't care to understand me at all. Anyway, I realized that the southern European tourist industry is based on this. Hordes of Latin lovers waiting like vultures for women, and despising them."

In 1959 money ran out and Barbara had to ask herself what she liked to do that might also earn her a living. The answer was unpromising, at least financially. She wanted to explore, to party, to inquire into the lives of other people. So she went to the BBC in London and told them that she met people easily and she'd be a good collector of interesting material. They had to be convinced—this was not the most professional of introductions. But they gave her a chance and she was good, as she knew she'd be. It was "just like breathing," she says. Of course, when the travel and the fun were finished, the other part loomed large and scary, the need to respond to the material, to organize it, and return it with the stamp of her name. "I sometimes wondered what I had to give back, and what right I had to muck about in people's lives. I don't know how you justify that, but over the years you do.

"I get very close to people with my tape recorder and I know how to hide a mike in the air. It's an obvious but secret weapon. I thought recently that I wouldn't take a tape recorder the next time I went out, but then I thought I'd never find out as much, and I wouldn't have done my research. I am there with a sign over my head that says, 'this person is interviewing you and she's going to ask you personal questions.' It's honest, admitting to a curious, snoopy nature, I guess. You really live a very full life and there are no commitments, which appeals to me. You get close, but you know you'll likely never see them again and that's sad, but a relief, too."

At the beginning, Barbara was a "wandering minstrel", she says, adventuring with the little black box and sometimes landing in strange places. Like the time in Spain when she was collecting gypsy music and found herself dancing on a table-top high in the mountains, holding a BBC microphone in the air long after the tape had run out because she knew that the man who had led her there would be expecting favours when the session ended. So the gypsies played into the night and Barbara danced, drunk on wine, laughing, shouting "for the BBC", until the man went home in the morning light.

It was lots of fun, but hardly professional. There were no assignments; she'd just take off, meet people, and put a piece together afterwards. One day she planned a trip to Ireland and decided to ask an experienced broadcaster at the BBC for tips about the country.

"What do you have in mind, young lady?" he asked.

"Well, I'm just going to mosey around," she said.

"Just in this for kicks?"

"Yes."

"Well, I'm not. I'm in this to make my living and turn out a professional job. And unless you want to wander aimlessly all your life, you'd better set limits and focus a bit."

Barbara heard him clearly and she never forgot his words.

Her work did become more focused and serious, but she continued to withhold part of herself, here as in her personal relationships. Never lay it all on the line was the unspoken credo. Then, if the result is less than excellent, if it is mediocre and disappointing and if the "big feelings" don't get expressed, there is comfort for the spirit in the thought that you hadn't put everything into it. Reserve a secret corner of talent to be tapped one day—maybe—because to lay it out and *fail* would be devastating. So Barbara has made countless excellent radio documentaries, many for CBC, where her skill at moving in close to her subject makes her work outstanding. She has made short documentary films for television. But she still feels "incomplete". "I've never *shown my face* in any of my work. I've never felt I've used my talents and my energies fully or well." The commitment, the complete investment of herself is still missing. It's like a hunger that never gets fully satisfied—still too much at stake.

At Christmas, 1964, Barbara returned to visit Toronto. She was 41 and still alone. Most of her friends were married and had children, and she found herself envying their closeness. She would notice couples on the street sharing conversation and she'd yearn for a partner, ignoring a persistent voice that whispered she wasn't capable of that. One night she went to a party feeling vaguely depressed. She met an attractive single man who interested her and she hung around hoping to leave with him. But he left with somebody else, and suddenly, there it was, as raw and hurting as anything had ever been. She walked home alone in the snow, drunk and crying, "Bellowing like a she-moose," she says, " 'you bloody lonely person, there must be something wrong with you because you are alone, you are alone, very alone. You're alone. YOU'RE ALONE. WHAT YOU HAVE ISN'T IT, NOT YET.'

"Part of the pain that night had something to do with not having a child, a feeling that I was not expressing the fullness of my body, my desires, my life. Sometimes I'd get pregnant— I've had several abortions. But those weren't sad times, because I never felt anything was a 'last chance'.

"I guess it's too late to have a child now, I'm probably in mid-menopause– ha! It's hard to know– but I keep taking the pill to remind myself that I'm damn well still a sexual being and I'm ready for any promising affair that comes along. Besides, having one affair breeds another. Like keeping in shape."

Barbara remembers crying through that painful night in Toronto and deciding in the blue cold of the morning that she would do something about her life. The conflict between the need to be free and the need to share her life had blown up like a gas balloon and spilled into consciousness, filling her with pain. "If I couldn't dare to open myself to another human being there was no point. I felt stuck, blocked, but I knew I wanted to open myself to life and be free to receive whatever came. I wanted someone to want me and I wanted to be able to want him."

She returned to England and psychotherapy. "I was helped to open up or dare to look needy or something like that, but I met a man almost immediately. He looked good to me and I thought, 'Oh, I like you, I'd like to see you again and I hope I do in my life' and he apparently thought the same thing.

"We were together six years and it was only through the help I got from therapy that I was able to sustain the relationship as long as I did. Somehow I learned to keep it going and to recognize that I wanted to, though it was so difficult and it didn't come naturally to me. I'd never lived with anyone on a long-term basis. I'd shared my bed over periods of time, but never truly shared a home. Suddenly I was part of a couple, two people living together, knowing each other, growing together, sharing things. I was anxious and demanding and difficult, but somehow or other I was very happy to be able to spend so much time in one relationship even if in the end it didn't continue."

It was an important time. Barbara felt happy; "Our relationship lacked passion, I think, but it was good and honest and we were comfortable together." But she is a restless woman; she needed growth and a dynamic rapport, while he was satisfied with a more static status quo.

"At the beginning I played house, like putting on doll's clothes. He made some demands, he wanted me to cook like his mother and his ex-wife. And he liked things a lot of men like—make-up, dressing up for him, my hair done prettily. . . . "

Barbara's a bit of a slob ("when you live alone you learn to be a *perfect* slob") and that's the way he loved her—at first. But then, when she was *his*. . . .

"I was forever yelling, 'What do you think I am; I'm not one of those dolls walking down the street—you should know that by now.' But he'd say, 'You could just do a little something for me.' So at a very late stage I grew to know what most women learn very early, the whole thing of being a housewife, and I must say it was a shocking education and I would *never* have understood what women are talking about today if I hadn't had that brief experience. I sometimes tried to do all these things, and I fed him and patched his clothes because I wanted to be with him, but eventually *he* began to notice that all my freedom, my madness, my energies were disappearing, and he found me less attractive. How ironic.

"One thing about batting around as a single woman most of your life is that you get to be fairly clear about which relationships are a bore and which are worthwhile. And none of them are truly worthwhile unless you take yourself and the other person seriously and decide that what you have is worth the risk of investing part of yourself in. But my husband and I lived like two gypsies, side by side. We never truly entered each other's lives.

"It was the big feelings again. I didn't know what to do with them in my marriage."

The other difficulty was that her husband was an antiquarian and made very little money. And he couldn't accept any from her. They couldn't visit pubs and have a crazy, laugh-until-you-fall-over good time with a grab-bag collection of friends, because he couldn't accept her money, neither under nor over the table. She hesitated about working at her radio interviewing or pursuing thoughts she had had of directing and producing films, because she didn't want to make him uncomfortable. He also wanted to make films.

That was a bad decision; it underlined just how far she had allowed her marriage to take her from herself. They grew apart and she returned to therapy, once again. "I thought there must be something wrong with me, Christ, I was still MISSING!!" This time she realized that there was nothing wrong with living the way *she* wanted to live, travelling, wandering, working hard, that she was not asking crazy things from her marriage and that her yearnings for intimacy and growth were not odd or unusual. "If I couldn't have a dynamic relationship with this man I knew I would have to do things on my own, as I always had." So they separated, painfully, she leaving her personal effects behind in "their" home, he taking another woman.

Barbara was already 46 years old and she had to fill, somehow, the ripped-edged gaping centre where her hope had been. She had spent a lifetime both chasing and escaping from what now seemed to be an illusion—couples and closeness. She spent six months in London, losing a grip on the edge of self-pity. Then the trip home to Toronto, in 1970, a visit to the coast of B.C. and a slow rediscovery of the source of early strength.

Work remained a problem as the self-discipline of freelancing became more and more difficult. Hello, Barbara? Sorry, she's gone to Spain. Hello, Barbara? Sorry, she's gone to Mexico. Hello, Barbara? Sorry, she's gone to the Yukon. The tape recorder was always in the packsack, but the work wasn't *serious*. Still, there remained the desire to "create something beautiful".

In 1973, when Barbara was 49, she was offered a chance to work for the National Film Board and make a series of films on women in the West. Now she wasn't sure. Did she *want* to take on such serious work? At this time in life, wouldn't she be happier doing good radio documentary work at her own pace, then hopping over to her cabin in Majorca for six months or so? Did she *need* the hours cooped up in editing rooms? Did she have the necessary reserves, the *urgency* to work hard enough to produce a good film, perhaps to stay in Montreal, learn another language, and compete with the bright talents of the Film Board who were young enough to be her children?

She decided to take a chance. I knew she would. And she made a sensitive film called *Ruth and Harriet* about two frontier women whose lives Barbara understood well. Many found her film authentic and moving. Her friends, of course, but also the critics.

Some months ago we sat in a subway car after an afternoon

of laughter and of trying on outrageous clothing in corner boutiques with back rooms that smelled sweetly of marijuana, and we talked about the move to Montreal, the strangeness of beginning a new career in middle age and the fact that Barbara was about to turn 50. Her eyes squinted under the harsh electric light and every part of her face seemed to move as she spoke. Her talk was non-stop that day, a flow of language punctuated by belly laughter. Talk on Toronto subways is usually conducted in somewhat muted tones, and even at rush hour riders endure the humiliations of sardine-like physical proximity with quiet composure. So her laughter attracted some critical attention. People turned to stare.

She said that she had only recently realized she has grey hair. Now I've known Barbara for five years and her hair has been grey at least since then, but *she* didn't discover the change until she looked at her film rushes one day and saw a silver-haired lady she didn't know. "I thought I was sort of ash-blonde," she roared.

"Sometimes I think my face is breaking up, but it won't. It just gets more interesting. But I guess it's a bit disturbing not to look as attractive as I remember. It has all come upon me quite suddenly." The laugh catches me off guard. I have prepared myself for tragedy.

"Sometimes I begin to wonder, though, who I'm attractive to now. I like younger men because they're more like me (though I have nothing against men of *any* age) and they like me for my spirit, though I sometimes wonder if they just like having a young mother along. Ha!" She laughed again. Barbara was high that day on good times and funny clothes and friendship. But I knew that the roar of her laughter was accompanied by a sadness.

I have had so little unconditional love in my life. Maybe I've given so little. I've sought a primary love, love of a parent, a man, a child of my body, and if there isn't one of these things in your life you can feel empty. I have felt empty though I have many friends. I went to the emergency ward of the hospital the other day and they asked for next of kin, are you married, whom do we call, I had nobody to give them. And that's what being single is all about.

"People always tell me to put something away for my old age, but I've never saved or had a pension plan or insurance or anything like that. I can't stand planning that sort of thing. They say, 'Barbara, you can't be an old lady running around with a tape recorder, sticking a microphone in people's faces,' but I know damn well I *can* be an old lady with a tape recorder, and I probably *will* be an old lady with a tape recorder. If I got ill I'd probably just get rid of myself, or get a damn good wheelchair and become a great writer."

I haven't been able to commit myself to an enduring relationship so somehow I have built the struts that hold my life together without the other supports, the close, living-together things. Either you're a failure or you're strong and tough, and that doesn't mean you're not sad or capable of gentle feelings and great loneliness. I have come to accept my own loveliness, too, and to realize that I attract loveliness in good, honest friends. But in the meantime, there's a lot of frail life, and I often feel I want to be looked after—just be dependent. Then I think, "Barbara, you shithead, just get on with it."

I'm a lot younger than Barbara but she makes me feel younger than I am. When I hesitate about whether I'll dare to do something quite different, I often think of her. And I usually decide to risk it.

"Getting on with it" is what her life has been and still is. What are the options? Men, for instance. There are fewer of them around now, and thoughts of female lovers hover in her mind as half-formed ideas. Why not? She has always had close female friends and now, with so many women alone because they have changed and grown and left their men far behind shouting angrily that they do not understand and are afraid to follow, so many women who have turned their heads inside out, and wrenched free only to discover that there *are* no men big enough to meet their still fragile newness with strength, tenderness, and respect, all those things, well then, why not? "Maybe it's a block or a fear," she says, "though I've thought of it. The experience might be deeply gratifying and if I ever met a woman I really felt that way about, I hope I'd be brave enough to try." Barbara's friendships with women have always been straightforward, stripped of the games and power plays men and women indulge in. "I become saddened and fed up with women who are not honest and depressed by all people who have stopped growing. I'm not as generous as I used to be, either. I'm critical, outspoken and impatient, and that's just fine."

Barbara's mother died some years ago and Barbara never did learn what life in Quathiaski Cove had meant to her. "I often wondered whether she had yearnings for something that was never quite fulfilled. I've felt her as a person of great sensitivity and gentleness and good intellect and I wonder what she would have done with her life if she had been born and lived at a different time."

"Then I remember the day she climbed to the top of the double-decker bus—just like a teenager. We looked out over the Thames and it was all sparkly and she grabbed me and hugged me. Then she said, 'Barbara, I love it here and now I know why you wanted to come.' She understood me—my yearnings—and she was tasting some of my joy."

Her father died in 1972, and when that happened, Barbara returned to the coast and boarded a ship that went up through the waters he had travelled. The ship stopped at lighthouses and she visited people as her father had done. She stood in the wheel house of the ship and looked out over the sea for hours, reliving part of his life and part of her life and putting the pieces together, the shapes of little girl longing to join him as his companion on the sea, consolidating both their lives. "I have always been a lover of the sea and this was my testimonial to him. To feel whole again and simple, to go with the rhythm of the waves. . . . " Taking the pilgrimage again, Little Christian's, perhaps, the name matters little. If we're lucky, the wheel turns full circle and brings us face to face with our beginnings.

"We never talked about that, but about a month before she died she came to visit me in London, for the first time. I took her to concerts and pubs and galleries. One evening we went to a concert of Victoria de Los Angeles. I looked at her during the performance and her eyes were shining and her face was flushed and I suddenly thought *of course, my mother is on stage— finally.*

Barbara's last decision was to stay in Montreal and make another film. "I don't want to do very big things. I want to make a few quiet, feeling poems and then a film that will show some of my edges." Who knows how long she'll stay. Two months, six years, ten years? "When I'm 60, I hope I'm having fun. I hope I'm with a nice man and that we're in bed a lot and eating good meals and drinking wine. I'll be in a big city making short sensitive films, I hope, or if that doesn't work I'll be in the bush with snowshoes, cooking a pot of beans on the stove. But I could go anywhere in the world and live a quiet life and discover writing and painting again. Who knows?"

The last I heard of Barbara, she'd gone travelling in the Arctic, with a tape recorder, a sleeping bag, and a bottle of rum.

Atwood In Metamorphosis:
An Authentic Canadian Fairy Tale

BY VALERIE MINER

I take this picture of myself
and with my sewing scissors
cut out the face.

Now it is more accurate:

where my eyes were,
every-
thing appears

The Journals of Susanna Moodie

Once upon a time there was a writer who played make-believe. She had many roles. And there was a journalist who came to take a photograph of the writer. The journalist could not find a good likeness because the writer mistrusted cameras and kept changing her image. So the journalist came away with several photos and she made a collage.

Margaret Atwood is the archetype of the elusive writer, used to submerging herself in her symbols and characters. A classic protean personality: woman, artist, academic, wild creature. A fairy-tale princess in her pre-Raphaelite hair and piercing blue eyes and Botticelli pink skin, running away from the wicked camera.

Snap: Drinking home-brewed beer and eating home-baked chocolate cake at the farm near Alliston, Ontario, where she lives and works. Feeding the chickens, tending the forest of indoor plants. The satisfied rural Ontario farm woman.

173

Snap: Frenetic hippie in Afro-auburn hair, blue jeans, and orange Indian overblouse sitting at a black Selectric typing out novels in an upstairs room. She is the recluse writer—laconic, brusque—the prodigy who won the Governor General's Award at twenty-seven, the literary celebrity of the moment at thirty-five.

Snap: The trenchant scholar. English instructor at Sir George Williams University, the University of British Columbia, York University. She is the respected literary critic and staunch apologist for nationalism orating at the Federation of Ontario Naturalists and the Empire Club. She spins out her sentences, catching her audience in her similes. Sardonically cool and professional.

Snap: The mythically free animal of her imagination. The six-month infant being carried into the Quebec North Woods; the teenage "nature girl" explaining frogs and toads to summer camp children; the university student more comfortable in the Lake Superior bush than in the Toronto classroom. She grew into the red fox-woman of her musings.

Snap: Successful, independent person who has made it with a strong sense of herself as a woman. Well-loved at home. Successful in her career. An example for the feminist movement, an ideal from whom all of us can draw confidence. She is a "role model".

But ultimately the role model identity fails, because in emulating her, we lose focus on our own strengths and we distort her individuality. I didn't realize it, but I was looking for an elusive self-image in Margaret. So the last photo is an optical illusion, because I was pointing the camera at someone who was standing in front of a mirror. When I developed the story, I not only had photographs of her, but pictures of myself taking the photographs. This piece is about Margaret and about me and about the two of us together.

In the spring of 1974 I took the CP over the Albion hills to ask Margaret why and how and where and when she writes.

And if I was eager to find a role model, she was equally anxious not to be found. Margaret's defensiveness is legend. She's revealed it on CBC programs, even in her conversation in *Eleven Canadian Novelists* with Graeme Gibson, the man she lives with and knows and trusts. Still, I was surprised when she proved to be the most evasive subject I have ever interviewed. It's easy to write about politicians or businesswomen or scientists or sorceresses because I don't want to be a politician or a businesswoman or a scientist or a sorceress. But I am a writer, and I was frustrated when Margaret didn't empathize with my standards and goals. Meanwhile, she had come to be wary of reporters arriving on the Vista Dome bearing cameras.

Margaret and Graeme pick me up at the station in their clanking, mud-streaked Rambler. As we drive over the hills to their small farm, we talk about the escalating price of alfalfa and oats, about the ominous threat of a commuter train piercing the privacy of Alliston. One reward for living fifty miles from Toronto is that people are inhibited by the long distance telephone charge. She shares a six-party line and only has to answer after one long and one short ring. "You have no idea how pleasant it is to know that the call isn't for you each time it rings."

She doesn't mind being a successful writer, but she does mind being famous. She never anticipated the money or the public recognition. She thought that being successful in Canada meant getting your books reviewed in the *University of Toronto Quarterly*. "But now I feel I can't be myself in public. People think that you're indomitable, invulnerable. They wouldn't think that about me if I didn't have this big reputation. *I'm* not intimidating. But because I'm a writer, people care whether or not I'm paying attention to them. They are afraid, in love, or hostile. They feel there are certain things they can't say or certain things they *have* to say, because only I *can* understand.

"Sometimes I would just like to be able to walk down the

street and have no one notice me. But in Canada people talk to me on the airport bus, while I'm taking a quiet pee in Eaton's, when I'm walking down Bloor Street." In the end, she says, it's all superfluous. "The only important thing about being a writer is what you write." That's why she admires Beatrix Potter so much. When she was tired of writing, she refused to talk to anyone about her work and started a sheep farm. Margaret toyed with the idea of raising cattle some day—until she tried it, and quickly tired of chasing escaped cattle through thunderstorms. Meanwhile, she carries around a "fetish" Graeme made for her—a small wooden figure saying "no" to the students wanting advice, reporters wanting interviews, editors wanting copy, and academics wanting lectures.

A writer has to invent a public persona or go underground. Alliston is on the road to Margaret's underground.

> When we were in it we were very small very
> small, at least we thought we were small
> and it was giant it was too green
> for us it was like living
> on the surface of the sun (green). . . .
>
> *Procedures for Underground*

The Kodachrome slides of Peggy and her brother Harold growing up in the woods show them paddling canoes, picking berries, bathing by the lake, chopping wood, catching pickerel for dinner. Carl and Margaret Atwood carried Peggy into the Quebec North Woods when she was six months old. The family spent half of each year in the woods—mostly in Northern Quebec—where Dr. Atwood did research in forest entymology. They lived in tents and rough cabins which they built themselves. According to Dr. Atwood, "Tradition has it that no hireling lays a finger on an Atwood operation."

Her Maritime background is important to her although she grew up in Quebec and Ontario. She is proud of the heritage of severity, frugality, honesty, hospitality, shrewdness—almost preoccupied with her roots. One of her ancestors was Cornwallis Moreau, the first white child born in Halifax, the son of a monk expelled from his order in France. The original Atwoods sailed over to Massachusetts in 1635 and later came to Canada before the Revolution. On her mother's side there were the Killams who arrived in Salem, Massachusetts in 1637. And there were family stories about the Websters and their descendants—Noah, the dictionary man, and the witch, who after she was hanged for casting a spell, got down from the gallows, cut the rope from her neck and walked away to live another eleven years. There was also the French Huguenot Louis Payzant who was killed in an Indian raid in 1756, four of his children escaping Mahone Bay to propagate and tell the story. . . .

Story-telling was an ancient, respected family tradition. Margaret Killam Atwood loved to read aloud from the Brothers Grimm and Beatrix Potter. Since their company was restricted to family, Peggy learned to be self-sufficient inside her imagination. Harold, two and a half years older, taught her to read when she was four. Together they wrote comic books. And they made up stories for each other when they went to bed, adding a chapter each night, radio serial style. Soon Peggy began to write for herself. Her mother remembers one night when Peggy was squirming into her pyjamas. "Hurry, Mummy. I'm telling myself a story and I can't wait to find out how it turns out."

In the woods outside their cabin Peggy enjoyed wheeling Buglie, the faded, eyeless panda bear around in a six-quart apple basket. For pets, Harold and she had the Canada Jays who ate out of their hands, the frogs, the toads, the snakes, the crayfish. When they grew older, they built an Indian tee pee out of birch bark and made maps of the woods, naming the uncharted lakes and rivers. Later, when a much younger sister had appeared on the scene, Peggy created fairy villages for her out of moss and lichens and stones.

Peggy was never treated like a little girl, but like a smaller person. You couldn't wear pink dresses into the woods—if you didn't have overalls and a healthy dose of her father's home-made Pyrethrum repellent, you weren't likely to survive the blackflies. Her mother wasn't a delicate female figure. She never liked housework, so she didn't mind living in tents or cooking outside. She never cared about clothes. Since her husband was away researching for weeks at a time, she took the children on wildflower hunts, picnics, and blue-berry-picking expeditions. "All my city friends thought my mother was horribly courageous. I just thought she was normal. I mean, we came from a long line of strong-minded women. The basic thing in a woman's development is how the parents treat the girl child. In Nova Scotia the image of the female is the hard worker, the good manager." Grandmother Killam went to Toronto from Nova Scotia to become a typist, which at that time was quite an adventurous thing to do. Aunt Kay was the first woman to earn an MA in history from the University of Toronto. Her mother's younger sister Joyce became a newspaper columnist. So the family didn't find anything peculiar about Margaret Killam Atwood's independence in the bush.

Margaret Killam, a vivacious tomboy, a rider of horses, was a little too fun-loving for her father, a country doctor, to send her to college. So she taught elementary school for a few years—riding her horse to and from classes—to save enough money to send herself to Mount Allison University. Meanwhile Carl Atwood, the son of a Clyde River, Nova Scotia saw mill operator, had gone to the University of Toronto to become a scientist. They got married and went off to the bush together in 1932.

But they never lost the Maritime heritage. Their daughter explains, "If I have any religion, it's a strong Nova Scotia moral code. We are against *waste* in all forms—from not wasting organic materials—I put it on the compost heap—to not wasting your talents or your time, to not wasting human life, which is why I'm against wars."

The Atwoods moved into the city each winter, from the first snowfall in October or November until the ice melted in March. The transitions—back to Ottawa and Sault Ste. Marie before she was six, afterwards to Toronto—were always dramatic. Peggy remembers her startling encounters with flushing toilets and sucking vacuum cleaners. But what alarmed her most was the way people changed their appearances; especially her mother, who put on nylons and dresses and hats and gloves and make-up when they came south. They had one identity for the city and one for the bush. She says now that the rhythm of going back and forth made her slightly "double-natured".

Peggy and Harold were different from the other kids. For one thing, they talked funny: complete sentences, precise grammer, Nova Scotia flat "A". They had been isolated from the slang of most childhoods. But what distinguished them most of all was their story-telling parents. The evening reading became a neighbourhood ritual. First a couple of friends asked if they could come over, then a few more started sitting in. Sometimes, the Atwoods had twenty children and tag-along parents sitting in their spare living room, listening to "The Tale of Benjamin Bunny" or "The House at Pooh Corner".

Another weird thing about the Atwood kids was their understanding of nature; Peggy had a pet cabbage butterfly and a praying mantis named Lenore. Dinner table conversation focused on topics like how long it would take a pair of fruit flies, multiplying unchecked, to cover the surface of the earth twenty-two feet deep. The kids were always reading from the bulging bookcases.

Peggy was a gregarious child. She was usually the youngest in the class, the fragile girl with the flushed cheeks and the clear blue eyes and the long dark curls, Botticelli even then. Her friends had heroines like Esther Williams and June Allyson, but her own were imaginary. And often they were animals; her first novel was about an ant floating down a river on a raft. She was "engaged" at age eight. She landed her first job that year: wheeling a baby carriage for twenty-five cents an hour. When she was eleven, she managed to knit an entire layette for her new sister Ruth. Several years later she was the hit of the neighbourhood when she opened her own puppet troupe and—for money—gave performances at birthday parties.

She says she didn't really have an adolescence. "I stopped writing from age eight to Grade Twelve. I consider it my sterile period," she says ironically. "I came into being when I was born. I had a temporary lapse in high school." The Leaside Collegiate yearbook portrays an All-Canadian girl: basketball team, UN Club, Citizenship Award. She belonged to the Triple Trio which went around to Rotary luncheons singing songs like "Come and Trip It As You Go". She entered the Unitarian Church in Grade Eleven, a dramatic philosophical commitment for someone brought up an agnostic. And she continued her eclectic employment career as a census taker, a waitress, a nature instructor at Camp White Pine "Where the sun forever shines", a Jewish co-educational camp in Haliburton. She concealed her intelligence in the classroom like most girls. Her early pioneer impulses were submerged in teenage anxieties about balancing on high heels. She shopped in Kresge's for her purple nail polish and orange lipstick. She made her own pastel formals for the school proms where she danced to "Tutti Frutti" and "Blue Suede Shoes".

But she also maintained a critical, defensive social and academic distance. "I was very sarcastic to people so they wouldn't mess around with me too much." She decided to major in home economics because of all the positions the guidance booklets suggested for girls—teaching, nursing, typing, homemaking—it seemed the most profitable and the least obnoxious. Once when she disliked her grade twelve home ec. assignment of making stuffed animals, she replaced it with an operetta about synthetic fabrics. (She wrote about Sir Wooley who had a blot on his character. He had to tell the girls Orlon, Rayon, and Nylon that he shrank from washing.) She claims that high school was just a walk-through for her—that she didn't develop the role seriously.

> She turned her head and examined her profile out of the corner of her eye. The difficulty was that she couldn't grasp the total effect: her attention caught on the various details, the things she wasn't used to—the fingernails, the heavy ear-rings, the hair, the various parts of her face that Ainsley had added or altered. She was only able to see one thing at a time. What was it that lay beneath the surface these pieces were floating on, holding them all together? She held both of her naked arms out towards the mirror. They were the only portion of her flesh that was without a cloth or nylon or leather or varnish covering, but in the glass even they looked fake, like soft pinkish-white rubber of plastic, boneless flexible. . . .

> *The Edible Woman*

"*The sexual awakening* wasn't that important to me. The only thing I regard as important was the moment I realized I wanted to be a writer. I even remember the first poem—about a desert. It was terrible. All my early poems were terrible, but that didn't matter. At that time I felt I couldn't get married and have kids and be a writer too. A pretty heavy acknowledgement for a sixteen year old girl. It seemed to me that getting married would be a kind of death. Society didn't provide alternatives then. There was no Women's Lib telling you that you could do both. I didn't feel guilty *as a girl* about wanting to write because at that time *no one* wanted to be a writer." But of course it wouldn't have mattered if anyone had objected. As her mother comments now, "No one guided Peggy. I don't think anyone could *guide* Peggy."

Carl and Margaret Atwood are still as bright and audacious

as that couple who took Peggy and Harold into the Bush. The house in Toronto where they have lived since Peggy was in Grade Three is spare, but warm. Durable tweed and naugahide chairs are set around a blazing fire. The mantle is clear except for candlesticks and cherrywood carvings made by Grandfather Killam. The hardwood floor is uncarpeted. Historical maps of Scotland and England hang unframed on one wall. Every open space is used for a bookcase or a planter. They see their daughter once a week on her treks into the city; they talk about books and Nova Scotia relatives and gardening. "We didn't intentionally raise Peggy in any specific way," says her father. "The marriage market just didn't make sense. Independence and freedom rate very high with us. One of the reasons we liked life in the bush so much was that it presented problems we had to settle without outside aid. We were on our own a lot."

Peggy got her first real recognition at the University of Toronto where she studied English with Jay Macpherson, Northrop Frye, Kathleen Coburn, Millar MacLure. She was an excellent student, was active in the drama group, and had male friends and boyfriends in spite of her seedy gabardine coat, her prim tortoise-shell glasses and the long, frizzy hair captured by bobby pins at the back of her head. The real hallmark of her college career was publishing—poems in *Acta Victoriana*, *The Canadian Forum*, *The Tamarack Review*. Most of her peers were indifferent about her writing ambitions, but she remembers one conversation with a date in the Toronto subway. "He thought it was all right for me to write, but to *publish*? His attitude was nothing new, in fact it was a hangover from the Victorian idea that there's something vulgar about a woman's name appearing in print. A lady is someone whose name is published three times: when she's born, when she gets married, when she dies. I didn't see why I should have to deal with that shit. A lot of women stopped writing because they felt this irrational guilt. I felt very alone, but I didn't feel guilty. Guilt just isn't my thing."

Nor is intimidation. When one of her University of Toronto professors advised that she be a wise girl and get married after her BA, she ignored him and applied to Radcliffe. She did her Master's and then moved over to Harvard for her Ph.D. She left school to write and to earn money to finish her studies. She taught at Sir George Williams and the University of British Columbia and York University. But she hasn't yet finished her thesis on the metaphysical romance. After she won a Governor General's Award for poetry in 1966, her writing began to absorb more and more of her time.

Other people were beginning to recognize what Peggy had known since that Grade Twelve poem, that she was a writer. Critics. Students. Reporters. They all asked why she wanted to write, "I don't care *why* I want to be a writer. It's such a Puritan question. It implies that you have to have some reason, some excuse to do something that isn't concrete. I suppose I've had my questions, my periods of severe depression, wondering whether it was any good, whether I could keep going, whether I was going to starve, whether I would live until thirty. But I never seriously thought I was going to *stop*."

Life with Graeme in Alliston is somewhere between the Atwood version of *Roughing It in the Bush* and her youth in the yellow brick house in North Toronto. Their old white farm house is the kind of unselfconscious home where the pipes are exposed in the half-formed bathroom, where *The Feminine Mystique* and *Canadian Dimension* are tossed next to the toilet, which only works when you descend your hand into the cold, murky waters of the tank and pull up the algae-covered plunger. The guest room is cramped with a freezer, sewing machine, fermenting bottles of homemade beer, and a dusty Zenith portable TV shoved behind two huge sacks of Vermiculite Garden Treat. The living room–dining room is the centre of activity in classic rural Ontario style—a cowgirl calendar from the Friendly Corner Store, a china cabinet with bits and pieces of place settings, a cupboard with a built-in flour sifter. We spend the evening sitting around the old round wooden table warmed by Graeme's hearty lamb stew, the wine, and the fire in the Franklin stove.

Margaret's relationships haven't always been so comfortable. In fact, most of the poetry she writes about men is troubled, heavy stuff: the exploited, martyred woman v. the uncommunicative distant man. The photos of high school and college were relatively easy to collect. But as we focus on the present, I find her backing away from the questions. She is close-mouthed about all her relationships. "The good ones I remember with gratitude. The bad ones I'm glad are no longer going on, but I can't talk about them. The people are still alive. It wouldn't be fair."

Margaret was raised outside the conventional bond between guilt and sex. She knew virginity was the bargaining point with most women in the fifties, but since she wasn't aiming at marriage, it wasn't an important asset. She did have one moral stricture—honesty, a directness which threads through her life. There were no patterns to her relationships with men—some were grizzly; some were good. Several engagements broke up because of her writing. "The men who didn't want me to write—who felt threatened by it—entrenched me in my belief that I wanted to write. Nothing else had as much meaning for me. It would be impossible for me to live with anyone who didn't allow me to be a writer. Repressing that part of me would lead to more misery than it would be worth. Tough for him. And for me. No one would have said to a man, you can't be a doctor, you've got to get married. I didn't see why I should give up writing. But it cost me a lot of blood, let me tell you. I missed out on a lot of things other women had—children, a husband for a long time. Now I know that I may not have missed anything at all. But the point is, I *thought* I did. It always hurt to say good-bye."

She didn't marry until she was twenty-seven. Not until, as

she had promised herself, she was a writer. She married a fellow Harvard graduate student. They separated in 1973 for what she says tersely were "personal reasons".

Marriage is not
a house or even a tent

it is before that, and colder:

the edge of the forest, the edge
of the desert
                              the unpainted stairs
at the back where we squat
outside, eating popcorn

the edge of the receding glacier

where painfully and with wonder
at having survived even
this far

we are learning to make fire

Procedures for Underground

Perhaps the most gossiped about of her private relationships was a rumoured affair with a young poet during the last part of her marriage, and which was reflected to some extent in *Power Politics*.

2
I approach this love
like a biologist
pulling on my rubber
gloves & white labcoat

You flee from it
like an escaped political
prisoner, and no wonder

3
You held out your hand
I took your fingerprints

You asked for love
I gave you only descriptions

Please die I said
So I can write about it

Power Politics

She used to be afraid of putting men down, but she doesn't submerge her talents any more. There aren't too many men who are secure enough not to feel intimidated by her. She says it's important to wait for someone who can handle it. Otherwise relationships are charades.

Life with Graeme is congenial, supportive, relaxed. Their work is similar enough to generate advice, different enough to obviate comparison. She insists that they're not in competition, that people who like Graeme's experimental novels would consider hers overly popular, a somewhat dubious assertion considering her critical acclaim. They go out of their way to ignore her reputation.

One evening after supper, Graeme entertains us by reading selections from the ever-proper *Pears Cyclopedia*. We laugh at the almanac's sensible advice on obesity, neurosis, masturbation, happiness. We spend the rest of the evening talking, and leave the dishes until morning.

"There's a lot to be said for my life right now. Here I am living with someone I get on with. I don't have to worry about money. I'm having a better time. I think I'd like to have kids; if I don't now, I never will. The 'purpose' of having kids is the same as the 'purpose' for writing. The theory is that you will enjoy it."

I sat in the house, raised up
between that shapeless raging and
my sleeping children
a charm: geometry, the human
architecture of the house, square
closed doors, proved roofbeams,
the logic of windows.

The Journals of Susanna Moodie

Her writing conveys a strong sense of female heritage, a spiritual, cultural kinship with other women. Her career is a statement of her confidence in herself as a woman. Like many pre-movement feminists, Margaret supports women's liberation, but it isn't the passion of her life. She never collected the linen or the children or the china, so she doesn't feel the real energy of bitterness that motivates many feminists. "Since I never felt my life was taken away from me, I don't have all that distilled outrage to devote to the movement. I don't mind playing roles—as long as I can determine the roles."

She notices a marked difference now in women's response to her work. She no longer senses the competitive hostility of those college cocktail parties where the girls always wondered why she wouldn't join them to talk about place settings. In fact women today are effusive in their encouragement. It is the men—those who used to pat her on the head and say, "Yes, dear, do go ahead and try to write," who feel threatened by her success. She says that she feels closer to women writers, that any rivalry is likely to take the form of wanting—or expecting—them to write better. She is more critical of women's work than of men's—more aware of their flaws and achievements.

Her books themselves could sustain a course on women's literature. *The Edible Woman*, a comic novel about Marian, a young college graduate who suffers Anorexia nervosa at the prospect of being contained in a marriage with a sterile young lawyer. *Surfacing*, a novel in which a young woman's search for her father serves as a metaphor for her search for sanity. *The Journals of Susanna Moodie*, a collection of reflections on the Canadian pioneer's life ranging from "The Disembarking at Quebec" to "The First Neighbours" to "Death of a Young Son by Drowning" to her resurrection as a contemporary old woman on "A Bus Along St. Clair". The other poetry collections are eloquent in their statement of female identity from the bitterness of *Power Politics* to the warmth of the poems about her mother and sister in *Procedures for Underground*.

Margaret writes about women simply because she is a woman. She says that she can empathize with, but not identify with male characters in books. She has no particular models. But perhaps her confidence derived from a youth immersed in Victorian literature: George Eliot, Christina Rossetti, the Brontës, Emily Dickinson. "The important thing is that women are right there in the foreground—you don't have to go out and dig them up. If they are *there* then you don't have to think it's curious that you're a writer. It doesn't matter so much what they write or what they are like personally, but just that they are there, so you know it's possible for you to be there too."

As we sit on the Mexican sun blanket which Graeme brought back from Oaxaca, she crochets white and blue and grey flowers. One after the other, alternating colours. She doesn't know what she will do with them—make an afghan or a coat or a . . . but she doesn't want to waste time. As I sit listening to her, I feel she is making pronouncements. She often interrupts questions, ignores ones she doesn't want to answer, answers ones she's not asked. I feel more like a disciple than a reporter.

This is not a unique reaction to Margaret. At parties, she's often the focus of attention, or adulation or hostility. According to one source, she has on occasion been known to sit and hold forth at length. Tonight, we're in one of those optical illusion scenes where I see as much of myself as I do of

Margaret. She laughs, "I guess this is kind of a defence. Like when I was sarcastic in high school. I still have some of the sarcasm left over. But my distance from people is more often disguised as wisdom of a spurious kind. Also, now people's attitudes toward me have changed so that those I meet usually want something from me. They don't give me the business, so I'm not as likely to give it back."

Her main aversion to radical feminism is that a didactic, one-dimensional critique will develop: women will praise women's books just because they are women's books, as a backlash to the predictably one-dimensional male reviews in which bad writing is somehow related to feminity and good writing is sexless or "male". "There's also the sexual compliment put-down, where a critic will comment on the cute cover photo and dismiss the contents of the book. A hard-hitting piece by a male writer is described as having 'balls'. But have you ever heard of work by a woman described as having 'tits'? Some feminists insist that my work, things like *The Edible Woman* and *Power Politics*, stem from the women's movement. But they didn't. This isn't to disparage anyone's politics. It is merely to indicate that parallel lines do not usually start from the same point and that being adopted is not, finally, the same as being born."

Margaret works in a small second floor study, just big enough for her huge desk, her bookcases, and a couple of chairs. The desk is cluttered with her thesis, with letters from her New York agent about the screen rights to *Surfacing*, with spray paint, a measuring tape, a bottle of Johnson's baby lotion. On one wall hang her own diffuse water-color paintings and a carefully executed sampler, "Blossoms and Birds and Budding Trees. Thank God We May Be Sure of These", made by her sister.

She is reluctant to discuss her work. She insists that her job is to write her poetry and fiction, not to do the definitive criticism of it. She does say that *The Edible Woman* expresses her own early fear of marriage and her distaste for the pompous, neurotic graduate student ethic. And *Surfacing* is set in the bush, written partly from childhood memories and subsequent observations. The protagonist, has a dominant, severe father; by contrast Margaret's father is affable, outgoing, fond of jokes, and energetic. "As far as what I've done, I'm more like my father, immersed in all sorts of projects and procrastinating about each one. Very rational. But spiritually, I think I'm more like my mother." As we talk, she digresses about her astrological sign, Scorpio, which is sceptical, and about her life-line, which has recently rejoined. "It would be quite possible for me to stop writing and go off in some opposite direction—something that would be an internalizing, rather than a pouring out. I think I have another life to live. . . . " She stops abruptly, as though concerned about gaining a public reputation as a purveyor of mysticism. She repeats that all she has to say, she expresses in her writing. It's her work that's important. Not her analysis of it or her personal life.

She bristles when I ask about the Yeats line, "How can we know the dancer from the dance?" "The only time a writer is in a dancer-dance situation is when he is writing the book. After that, it's cut loose, sent out. You change. I'm not the same person I was when I wrote *Surfacing*. The only thing that makes a book tolerable is the thought of finishing it. The final connection is between the reader and the book. You get a whole other sense of the work if you think of it as a thing apart from the author."

"Simplistically, any writer writes biography. But on a more subtle level, you also act like a lens, a movie camera. I project my energy into my characters. I'm not writing down the story of my own life, but I'm imagining myself in certain situations in which I haven't been before. Fictions are possibilities."

They can't be trusted. They'll mistake me for a human being, a naked woman wrapped in a blanket: possibly

that's what they've come here for, if it's running around
loose, ownerless, why not take it. They won't be able to
tell what I really am. But if they guess my true form,
identity, they will shoot me or bludgeon in my skull and
hang me up by the feet from a tree.

Surfacing

Margaret has been intrigued by metamorphosis since her
childhood. Animals are a form of mask. Another role. Another
image. Another identity. Wilderness is a pervasive theme in
her work. So is madness. Both wilderness and madness are
retreats from a pressurized world which threatens to contain
or manipulate. Escapes from claustrophobic urban life.
Disguises.

She still feels more at home in the Quebec bush than she
does in the streets of Toronto. She goes canoeing every year,
and she is an honorary member of the Federation of Ontario
Naturalists. She still talks about moving farther away than
Alliston once her career settles down. Margaret spends most
of her days on the farm with Ruby, the ancient matriarchial
tabby and Patience, the precocious black Persian, two Irish
Wolfhound pups and the ducks and the chickens and the sheep
and the peacocks. The animal she identifies with most is the
red fox. Some friends insist that she's a silver fox or an otter
or a hare. But the image is consistent: clever, quick, sprightly.
Her very appearance flouts urban sensibility. She dashes
around to Toronto editorial offices in blue jeans and loose
Indian overblouse, her electric hair coiling from her scalp, her
skin just washed and flawless except for those forehead lines
that the Atwoods seem to be born with. It's quite a metamorphosis from that prim young student in the muted wools who
pulled her hair back in a frizzy French roll. She looks like the
untamed creatures of her poetry.

Another escape-retreat from the claustrophobic rationality
and sterile stability is madness, a theme she explores in much

of her work. She has a neurosurgeon's skill with her succinct, terse sentences. She creates an individual dream world in which change and reorder are a nebulous constant. It is a universe where people drift in and out of madness, where the reference points between sanity and insanity are always shifting. One critic acutely described her as "a psychological iconoclast". Madness and wilderness come together in the animal fantasy of *Surfacing*. The protagonist goes through a role of a wild animal to distance herself from the neurotic people around her and to get in touch with her own fears.

Margaret's personal fear is chaos. "It's triggered off by having to deal with a lot of shit from other people. Sometimes I think I'll never get out from under it." She also tries to avoid situations in which she can be contained or limited by other people's expectations, political, moral, literary. "One thing you don't seem to grasp," she tells me in an irritated tone one day, "I don't think in terms of 'usual' and 'unusual'. *Of course* it was unusual for me to do a lot of things I did in other people's terms, but not in mine."

Her sense of stability is an individual one, distilled by her early experiences in the bush. In her life she keeps a fine balance between urban culture and natural environment. She still mistrusts machines and is only now learning to drive. When she flies, if she is close to completing a book, she will mail a copy of the manuscript to her home address in case the plane crashes. She describes herself as "depressingly sane. I've had it checked out. I went to a therapist when my marriage was breaking up, mainly to talk over things like how long I should keep the house. After a while, he asked me what I was doing in therapy. How I feel depends on the circumstances. When things are OK, I'm OK. If they're not, then I'm not. I'm very susceptible to input. That's why I moved out of the city. There was too much input."

"I think madness is a kind of escape valve in our society. It is symbolic of whatever is bothering a person. Our society makes it easier for women to crack up. Women are taught to fear, to think they need refuge, to believe they need to be taken care of. It renders them childlike and helpless." In *Surfacing*, she leaves it open to the reader whether the protagonist is crazy, or right, or crazy and right.

> In the evening I make a different lair, further back and better hidden. I eat nothing but I lie down on the rocks and drink from the lake. During the night I have a dream about them, the way they were when they were alive and becoming older; they are in a boat, the green canoe, heading out of the bay.
>
> *Surfacing*

The collage is finished. A composite of disparate images. Some more sharply focused than others. Some candid. Some posed. Some double exposed. No one representative. Duck eggs and crocheted flowers and fairy tale figures and mad women. Metamorphosis in the bush and metaphysical romance. The Connecticut witch's descendant. The child pioneer. The contemporary celebrity. As for the future . . .

Who is Margaret Atwood? The mirror cracked a long time ago and I still don't know. I climb on board the CP to take me back to Toronto and my typewriter. She gets in the old Rambler and heads back along the mudruts to her tower in Alliston. And if she doesn't live happily ever after, at least she knows that every time the phone rings, it's not for her.

> (The photograph was taken
> the day after I drowned.
>
> I am in the lake, in the center
> of the picture, just under the surface.
>
> It is difficult to say where
> precisely, or to say
> how large or small I am:

the effect of water
on light is a distortion

but if you look long enough,
eventually
you will be able to see me.)

The Circle Game

Hi, I'm Barbara Frum

by HEATHER ROBERTSON

She has a great voice, low, and warm, and sensual, a worldly voice with an edge of innocence, a knowing, suggestive voice that's full of laughter. "I find myself almost physically in love with everyone on the phone," says Barbara Frum. "I empathize with everything. I try to put myself into their heads. What they're feeling, I'm feeling too. I really get off on it." She is an uncompromising, tenacious, and indefatigable seductress. "There's not a moment when I'll say, 'Let that pass, so what,'" she says. "I see every day as the first day and the last day. I am unyielding."

Nobody puts much over on Barbara Frum. Her passionate curiosity has made the CBC's nightly phone-out show *As It Happens* the most influential national radio program in the country. She's smart and stubborn and suspicious. If you want to know what's *really* going on around the world, Barbara will try to find out, and if she doesn't always get the right answers, she asks the right questions. "I have a stern mind," she says. She also has an acute ear for lies and hypocrisy ("That's *bullshit*," she'll say vehemently, flicking off her microphone and mugging a face of disbelief through the studio window) and utter contempt for anyone who tries to manipulate her. Her questions are thoughtful, pointed, and unpredictable. She stalks her quarry with the skill and finesse of Sherlock Holmes, always polite, always respectful, always one jump ahead, feeding her guest enough rope to hang himself until she moves in, solves the crime, exposes the villain, and unravels the

195

mystery for her delighted audience.

"I'm fascinated by motive, *why* people do things the way they do. Stories are sometimes proposed to me in a very simple conspiratorial way. It's been my experience in life that things are always a lot more complicated than that." She is sensitive to ambiguities, aware of nuances of voice and hidden meanings in words. She concentrates intensely on what each person is saying, and on what he is leaving unsaid; she tunes in to the vibrations of fear and anguish and rides the emotional undertow.

"There are some issues that get me in my gut and some for which I feel no emotion at all. Simple stories just bore me. Somebody split an atom. Terrific. He found a new particle. Wonderful. Good for you. I'll get up for them, I'll say hello and congratulations but I don't get *steamed*. I get steamed about current issues where there's a decision to be made, and I really get steamed about stories where *I don't know what really happened*. That's when I really get excited! There's *more*, there's *more there*! I always love it when things aren't the way they seem."

Barbara's love of drama has influenced the muckraking style of *As It Happens*. The nightly bag of stories is a combination of scandal, spy thrillers, political machination, gossip, and adventure leavened by assorted freaks, mad inventors, pirates, and iconoclasts. Most of the stories are chosen by the producer, Mark Starowitz, and the editors; few of the ideas are Barbara's. "They'll come at me with a story and I'll go along or I'll balk," she says. " 'Wooo,' I'll say, 'No way! Come on. Stop. Give me a minute and let me argue with you.' " The producers know what she's a sucker for. "The Patty Hearst thing—they teased me unbelievably! Once a day they'd throw Barbara her Patty Hearst story. Keep her happy in her cage. Stories like that absolutely wow me."

Tantalized by a whiff of duplicity or corruption, Barbara will return like a bloodhound to the scent. "They laugh at me because once a day I say, 'This story stinks. We've got to do more on this. There's more here. I *know* it!' I let a cabinet minister get by me about two weeks ago, and I couldn't forgive myself all night. Incredibly the next day there he was again, and I could grab him. That's why I love the program, because I get a chance to go back. Every night I can correct my mistakes. I'm not sloppy or careless, I don't say, 'What the hell, I don't care if I've got that right.' I care intensely about getting things right."

As It Happens is real-life soap opera, a serial melodrama replete with pathos, passion, and human frailty. Its listeners are hooked on this fleeting nightly exploration of the human condition, fascinated by the unexpected revelations, the twists of plot, the confrontations between good guys and bad guys, the spectacle of real people stuck in tough spots. Barbara flies by hunch and intuition, full of compassionate understanding for the small personal agonies she is probing. She listens. People trust her. They talk.

"There are few emotions that I can't feel in myself," she says, "and there are very few ugly emotions in myself that I haven't expressed or dealt with. To that extent I consider myself a liberated person. If somebody tries to give me what's on the surface, it doesn't make sense to me. So I go deeper." She's not mushy or sentimental and she doesn't let anybody off the hook when things get rough.

"I am no respecter of place at all. I have no respect for authority whatsoever. I have respect for individuals and how they're coping with politics but I won't say, 'Your lordship minister sir, can I kiss your bum!' No! And I'm amazed at interviewers who do. I've always despised the interviewer who will kick around Joe Shlunk over there and let a cabinet minister walk in and it's 'How do you do sir, such a privilege to meet you sir.' I just can't bear that. It was the situation in which I grew up. There was just never any need to kiss anybody's ass *ever* in my life and I just *won't*. The funny thing is that I don't share a lot of general cynicism about politics.

It's not that I assume everybody's a crumb. It's just that I assume everybody's a human being with a pair of legs until I hear otherwise. Whether you're a premier or a prime minister or whatever, inside there you're just the same quivering piece of meat that I am."

People find it hard to believe that Barbara Frum ever quivers. Her honesty and her poise have made her one of Canada's most respected and feared interviewers. "People tell me I'm formidable," she says. "Actually I'm a latent patsy. They won't see my pain. They just see my strength. To some extent I'm the prisoner of other people's expectations." She is cautious in her dealings with strangers, jealous of her dignity and reputation. She won't do commercials ("Hey, Murr," she'll shout to her husband, blowing in the door, "you're looking at Mrs. Pepperidge Farm!") and she doesn't market herself by discussing her sex life and recipes with reporters from women's magazines. She understands how easily she can be victimized by her public, especially by other women who, motivated by envy and malice, could attack her to enhance their own reputations or could trade on a fraudulent bond of sisterhood to hold her up to judgment and ridicule. She has no use for "true confessions" journalism or for the feminist reporters who demand that women tell all to satisfy the voyeurism of their readers, yet who never make the same demands of men. She knows how easily she could be ripped off, because she's done it to others; she is still upset about a cruel profile of celebrities' wives she wrote for *Maclean's* several years ago. "I'll never be able to choke back the feeling that I as a woman exploited other women," she says. "At the moment the story seemed important. Now it doesn't. Some of those women were my friends, and what really bothers me, I guess, is that they might have told me those things as a favour." She wants to know my motives in interviewing her. Am I going to hold her up to a pattern of feminist virtue and see whether she fits? Am I to decide whether Barbara Frum is good or bad, honest or corrupt, a success or a failure? "It's pompous to talk about yourself," she says. "Everything sounds so banal." She pauses for a moment, then her eye gleams. "But I must admit I'd like to know how people like Golda Meir and Indira Gandhi *really* got where they are." Because she makes her living asking people questions she respects their right to ask questions of her. It's fair. But she flatly rejects their right to pass judgment on her.

"A week or so ago I was suddenly confronted by a woman who had expectations of me that I couldn't fulfill. It scared me. I made some remark at dinner, I can't even remember what it was, and she threw down her knife and fork and said, 'Barbara, how can you say such a thing?' It was like someone had thrown cold water in my face. Who the hell is she? How dare she decide what I should think? I was to play the role of objective interviewer even in my own life."

She is still disconcerted at losing her anonymity. "I never expected people to stop me in the supermarket. I get quite excited. Very childish. I'm so pleased that they like me. I never imagined my life making any difference to anybody else. A reporter asked me the other day 'What have you got to say to the women of Canada?' Good God, the women of Canada! Hi!"

Because of *As It Happens'* radical political stance people tend to assume that Barbara's a Marxist. She's not. "I'm a liberal. I'm not for the destruction of capitalism or private property. I think that society should be efficient, productive, smart, and responsive. Every inning should be a wide-open chance. I have no use for armchair radicals. The best I can do is make available to people the kind of knowledge and approach to make them aware of the system they live in—*why* did it have to happen that way?" Barbara Frum is rich. Her husband Murray is a Toronto real estate developer; she drives a Jaguar and lives in one of the most magnificent homes in Toronto. She has a live-in housekeeper five days a week and spends spur-of-the-moment weekends in Florida. Barbara's clothes are elegant and expensive; she always looks dressed-up, a girl of the Fifties who grew up in a girdle. "They call me 'fancy lady' at the CBC," she laughs. " 'Different outfit every day.' " Yet she always has the slightly frazzled, helter-skelter look of a woman who works hard and isn't vain. She is tall and slim with thick black hair cut in a long shag, high cheekbones, and a stunning smile, the kind of woman whose beauty lies in her radiant energy. Barbara makes no apologies for her life style.

" 'She's privileged,' people say. Well, I *am*. I wouldn't want to try to be anything else. It's a matter of knowing your place. That's what I am. I might as well see it through and take my lumps." She takes a lot of lumps from people who can't reconcile her social conscience with her social status and who think she has no right to come on the radio as Mrs. Joe Canada. Yet in her pragmatism, conservatism, and capitalism Barbara represents the aspirations, and ultimate achievement, of middle-class Canada. "I'm very square, very conventional," she shrugs. "All I can do is give people the benefit of my honesty and take my chances."

Barbara identifies frankly with her listeners. She talks Canajan, a slangy, vivid, colloquial jargon that instantly puts people at ease and gains their confidence. "I swear too much," she says, and she laughs a lot. Her favourite expression is a hushed and reverent "Wow". Most of her interviews are pre-recorded and ruthlessly edited to heighten the tension and eliminate flat spots. She makes brilliant use of silence, turning off her microphone to edit out her own gasps, giggles, and mutterings. It has a devastating effect on her guest who, faced with emptiness at the other end of the telephone line, babbles on frantically to fill the void. "You develop a style," she says. "Nothing is contrived, nothing is conscious. I like to think that I'm better now. It's been a gradual stripping away. I used to be more aggressive, more black-and-white. I've come to realize that the interviewer should not become the issue. I get very upset if I feel that I've talked too much. If I get stranded it means I've become the subject of the interview, and that was a mistake." She is intimate and relaxed and will talk away confidentially to people who would leave the rest of us parched and tongue-tied.

"I had a nice chat with the Queen," she says. "I even got a laugh out of her. I was really proud. I ended up quite liking her. She's in a tough spot and she does a good job. She's a committed woman and I came away with some admiration for her, even though I think it's awful that she has to wear those terrible clothes and do those awful things. I pity her. No, that's stupid. I don't pity her. That's wrong because I think she could have a pretty cushy thing there, but she's too middle-class to enjoy it. Underneath it all is a very compulsive middle-class woman and not at all an aristrocrat. She has no *grace*, she has no real dignity. She's just a working girl. She's very tedious. I wouldn't want to spend a lot of time with her."

Barbara's evaluation of the Queen reflects her own respect for work, for duty, for grace under pressure. She goes through life like a buzz saw. "People think I'm compulsive," she says. "I'm not. I'm a real firefly. I crave so many things that the pace of my life suits me. I love it. I'm thoughtful, but I'm not an intellectual, I'm not someone who lives with ideas. I'm very curious, very energetic. I can take a lot of tension, a lot of pressure. I kind of think, Barbara, what the hell, you're doing as well as anyone could, and who else could take it anyway?"

She spends almost eight hours a day in the hot, cramped recording studio she calls her "cage" where, earphones strapped across her head to pick up the constant chatter of instructions from her producer, she fires questions into the microphone. She'll go through 15 interviews a day; those that don't work are thrown out. (Barbara won the CBC's "Worst Interview of the Year" award in 1974 for one in which her guest answered every question with a curt "No".) She prepares conscientiously for each conversation and gives it her undivided attention; she won't slide by with a cheap cliché or muddle along burbling platitudes or take up valuable air time with gumflapping. She has an urgent sense of time; she doesn't waste hers or anyone else's. "There are no bogs, no slack," she says with satisfaction. "It's a completely efficient use of me. When I get home I have no guilt that I didn't do anything today." Once a week she tapes a one-hour television interview which is broadcast over the CBC's Toronto station Tuesday night at midnight. The show is called simply *Barbara Frum*. She writes occasional articles for *Maclean's* and does interviews for the Ontario educational TV network. All her work requires enormous concentration and intellectual energy.

"I can get very exhausted," she admits. "I can get so tired my face feels frozen, but I can lie down for a short while and really go again. There are some nights when I'll be running around the house at 2 a.m. and my husband will say 'Barbara, will you lie down! Will you sit down already!' " Behind Barbara's daring and confidence, structuring her ironclad judgments and ruthless pursuit of the truth is a merciless conscience.

"I am very afraid of judgment," she says. "I'm very self-critical, I'm very pained by criticism. I take it very hard, my own as well. I can really mutilate myself with my own judgment of my own work." The pace of her life is, to some extent, flight. "I can forgive myself for a mistake because I've probably done 12 things okay today," she says. "I don't think I could take doing a book; working towards a climax of judgment would absolutely kill me."

Her self-assurance is based on a realistic assessment of her strengths and weaknesses, of where she stands in relation to other people. She's not invulnerable. "What would stagger me," she says, "is a live face-to-face interview with someone I really respect. That would throw me, terribly. Because if I couldn't do an interview that was worthy of that person, it would bother me. I can't bear to talk to people whose books

I haven't read. It's not fair. How dare I grab a piece of them? Or someone whose life is their work. Someone who lives a good life and who makes some kind of meaning of their life, who makes their time on earth say something. Not someone who has just *done* something spectacular, but someone who is living something. That throws me. And movie stars throw me. Absolutely. If I see Anthony Quinn in a hotel in Paris my mouth drops. I'm staggered. I don't know what to say to a movie star."

Barbara can be critical and contemptuous of people she considers phoney or corrupt; she can be devastatingly funny at the expense of fools, but she is not callous. She doesn't use people as grist for her personal mill. And she expects the same treatment from everyone she deals with.

"I don't want to be used. I hate a story that's exploitive. It drives me *wild*. When someone wants me to debate the Jewish Defence League I won't do it. It plays bread and circuses with something I think matters a lot. I won't use news or events as entertainment. And I won't be used myself. I am extremely sensitive about affairs that deal with Jews. I don't manipulate the news and I don't want my Jewishness manipulated for the entertainment of a TV audience who will just say, 'Oh well, there are the Jews fighting.' I am very conscious that I have a position of enormous privilege and I'm very self-conscious about how the audience sees me using the platform power that I have. I don't want to abuse it. You can bend over backwards so far that you become an enemy of the Jews, an enemy of your own people, in order to show the Christian world that you're fair-minded. It's sort of like a woman saying, 'Anyone can make it. I'm not going to express myself as a woman because that's just being a victim. It's just saying I belong to a minority class. If I pretend the women's issue is not an issue it will go away.' A lot of Liberal Jews got trapped like that. They tried to play it the gentile way, the Christian way, they tried to ignore it. It's the only issue I'm sensitive on. It *matters*. The survival of the Jewish people matters to me. And at the moment it's debatable whether they will survive or not. A lot of people don't understand how vulnerable the Jews are. There have been people who have disappeared off the face of the earth because the great powers decided. That's the position I see Israel in. And I condemn Israel every time. They have done awful things, *awful* things. I'm not a jerk about it. And I'm not defensive about public relations things. A Jew can be as big a fool as anybody else. I couldn't care less."

Barbara Rosberg was born in 1938, the eldest of the three children of Florence and Harold Rosberg, owners of Rosberg's Department Store, the biggest department store in Niagara Falls.

"People expected a lot of me," she says with a little sigh, as if the memory of her childhood was one of hard work. "They made incredible demands of me. It was because my father was one of the wealthiest men in a small town. He made himself into a 'good' man. He gave to charities. He was painfully shy but he sat on committees and forced himself to make speeches at meetings. It was noblesse oblige. I was very conscious of that. Always I was a complete outsider. 'You're different,' people would say. I remember at school one day standing around with a bunch of my friends, chewing gum. A teacher came down the hall and said, 'Oh Barbara, not you!' I really was isolated. People had extreme expectations of me. Maybe they pushed me too hard.

"My parents didn't demand that I be brilliant. I always used to win the effort awards. 'You're a plugger, make the most of your gifts.' I used to enter oratorical contests at school. One part of me would volunteer—and then the panic! My parents wouldn't let me back out. 'You stay in. You can't quit. It's good for you!' The contests used to be held on parents' night, with 800 people sitting out there in the auditorium. It was exquisite agony—and I used to win. I'd be in the money. You learn something from that."

As she talks I am astonished by the similarities between us

(I can see myself again in my white middy standing in the pulpit of the candlelit church reading chapters of Matthew in a high, nervous voice at the CGIT Christmas service, stiff with fear and self-importance) and by how little differences of race and religion really mean in this country. She, a Jew from southern Ontario, and I, a WASP from the prairies, are both children of the Depression, daughters of intelligent, energetic mothers whose own ambitions were bent by poverty and social custom into the mold of conventional domesticity.

"My mother was the power in the house," says Barbara, "and my grandmother had been the power in the house before her. I am the third generation of a really matriarchal family." She speaks with finality, as if that's all that needs to be said. And it is. I know what she means. I come from a matriarchal family, too. I wonder how many of us who are driven to be powers in the world carry that burden of responsibility towards our mothers and grandmothers and great-grandmothers who taught us to be smart and strong and self-reliant and not to take as much shit in life as they did. Are we living their lives out, too, fulfilling their ambitions as well as our own, propelled by their vicarious energy, anger, and frustration? The little empire of husband and children isn't big enough any more. We are trying to get out of the house, to break through the bell jar of middle-class boredom, to live, if only by telephone, in a world larger and more exciting than the neat and tidy universe of respectable girlhood in which we grew up. We are daughters of the bourgeoisie, protected, prosperous, shaped by the decorum of the home and the discipline of the public school which taught us to compete, and win, serious people aware of the hope and sacrifice invested in us, conscious of the risk and fear of failure.

"I was born an adult," says Barbara. "I had a real sense of waiting my time. I knew I was a person inside and they just didn't see it. It wasn't until I got married that I was recognized as being the adult I was."

Barbara and Murray Frum have been married 18 years. "We feel like a couple of old crones hobbling around on our sticks," she laughs. "Our lives have fused together into an encrusted thing, a rock that's got seaweed and barnacles on it and crevices with mollusks living in them. Our marriage is not an issue, it's not something you pull out of a drawer and reassess every so often. It's not debatable. There are no judgments being made, ever. The package was bought whole—there are no untidy corners that we hide from ourselves or each other."

She married at 19. She was a student in Arts at the University of Toronto, Murray was a 25-year-old dentist. "We've changed," she says. "What I don't understand is how we anticipated our *now* selves and were so right when most people seem to have made a mistake." She finished her degree after her marriage, then her son David, now 14, was born.

"I was happy as a clam," she says. "Nobody can believe it. I was blissfully happy, just completely enchanted with being a mother and taking care of that child and entertaining friends and going out to dinner. I had never thought about a job. I was heading into being a very scientific wife and mother. That's what my mother had done. I read, I studied, I intellectualized what my child was doing. I felt that what I was doing was really worthwhile. And I was very good at it. I could really cook. I could make good choices. I was extremely good at being a mother. I had all kinds of energy. I was very competent and very successful."

She reminds me of all the girls I knew who quit university to get married at 18 or 19, intelligent, self-possessed, well-to-do girls who married doctors and lawyers and dentists. They all had two or three children and played bridge and drove their own cars and looked very chic and fashionable. They joined the Junior League or Hadassah and raised money for the symphony and art gallery. They read widely, studied sociology or art history at university, and took up Indians or emotionally disturbed children or day care. They worked hard on their husbands' political campaigns, cooked gourmet dinners, and wrote briefs to the government. They were formidably organized, productive, and took everything very seriously. Yet they never seemed to get anywhere. Ten, fifteen years later they're still wearing the same clothes, studying the same subjects, promoting the same causes, unable or unwilling to make the imaginative leap that will keep them from turning into their mothers.

Barbara finds it hard to relate to her old self, or to understand how and why she made that leap. "I always knew I'd do something in the world," she says. "But I never had any plan. I just backed into it." Her first job was a radio talk for CBC *Matinee* telling mums how to amuse their kids. It was 1963 and she made $35 a week. She bought a tape recorder. "I'll do whatever you want," she told producers. Through a friend she stumbled on a story about corruption in the TB seals campaign and sold it to the Toronto *Star*; within two years she was working full time as a journalist and broadcaster. In an era when female interviewers were supposed to be sweet, blonde, and silly, Barbara's tough, unrelenting, aggressive style shocked her audience and her employers; in 1971 she was fired from the CBC's Toronto public affairs show *Weekday* because management considered her questions "too tough". "I've taken a lot of rejection," she says matter-of-factly. She doesn't dwell on it. In the five years she's been with *As It Happens* she's won every award available for excellence as a radio interviewer and has helped revolutionize the image of women in broadcasting. "Nobody's asked me to be president of the CBC," she says, "but if they did, I'd say yes."

Barbara makes no distinctions between her work and her life. "I have good feelings about my life matching," she says. "I'm not escaping into my work, back home is not a lingering chronic indictment of my life." Her marriage, her children—David, Linda, twelve, and Matthew, seven—her home, her wealth, her strong sense of "place" give her the security and protection she needs to be free, to experiment and explore. "We live a completely improvised life," she says. "There's almost no structure." Since Murray gave up dentistry he has adapted his schedule to Barbara's; the whole family has dinner together every night at 8 p.m. when she gets home. The children call their parents by their first names; they are independent, outspoken, and direct. "I don't quite feel like their mother," says Barbara. "I feel like some person living with them. We've never lived for the sake of our kids, we've always lived our own life. We've both got a real sense of the shortness of life. That's one thing Murray learned from me. Do it now. Indulge your feelings now. Eat that meal *now*. Don't save, don't wait, don't bank on tomorrow. So we live our lives completely according to the moment. I'm beginning to fear for my children that we haven't built enough structure into their lives. I sense maybe there's a craving for ritual we haven't provided. Our kids can't remember when we've *always* done something. I think maybe we've let them down. The truth is that we've never been willing to sacrifice our lives for them. I don't know if that's good or bad. We've each harnessed our lives to such an extent that to harness what little time we have together seems insane, and to spend the time we can have together in the service of our children never made much sense either. But I consider that selfish of me. So I feel I'll get docked by God for that, but I'm not willing to stop. I don't defer for the future what I can have today, and I'm taking pot luck about tomorrow."

There is nothing masochistic or self-destructive about Barbara's highly public life; she has a strong sense of privacy and self-defence. "I don't like people to have something on me," she says. "If I ask a question that gives a guy a hammer to bang me over the head with, then that's a lousy question. I'm upset if someone thinks I've made an error in judgment. I guess it gets at my essential vanity. Or if people criticize me physically. I don't care about myself physically, but I think I get away with it, you know, and that one time I didn't. If I see that I'm sitting in a chair awkwardly, that will bother me, or if my hair makes me look like a monkey. I love provocative clothes but I only wear them at home. I don't want to cause notice."

She is sensitive to where she stands in relation to other people and to their feelings towards her: are they ally or invader, friend or foe? "Sometimes I can be completely indifferent to my harm, and other times very self-conscious," she says. "I am intensely vulnerable. People are frustrated by the fact that I don't have any sense of myself. They want me to have a better sense of who I am. I have to divide my life up into pieces. A man lives a total existence. He can get out of bed and into his suit, and until that suit comes off at night he's . . . John Robarts. Did you ever look at a man in a beautiful shirt and tie and think that as long as he's in that casing he knows who he is? I go home and I change modes. At home the president of the Toronto Dominion Bank is still the president of the Toronto Dominion Bank.

"Some days I feel I'm a paler version of myself. Take Adrienne Clarkson. There's a woman who's total. She always has a last name. She always has a sense of herself, so that when she goes out the door she's playing the Adrienne Clarkson Story and she's the star of it."

But, I say, isn't that essentially alienating?

"Sure," she says. "You're right. But for the person who can pull it off it must be very satisfying. I guess what I'm craving is a little more alienation, so I won't be so full of my flaws and so full of my mistakes, and won't penalize myself so heavily. I guess I have a lingering admiration for people who can kid themselves a little bit better because I think sometimes they're a little bit happier. The people who know just the right jam for breakfast I think are wonderful! I love people who eat the same marmalade for 20 years. There's a kind of coziness to it.

People who always have a leg of lamb on Sunday."

Barbara describes herself as a "cultural Jew". "I believe in God only as fate, the ongoing context in which we live and die. I saw a cartoon once. A man was asking God 'Why me?' and God replied 'Why not?' That could be embroidered in needlepoint and hung up on my wall. I believe in goodness as an entity, something to be striven for, but if you think that this universe is good and the good are rewarded, you're crazy. It's temporary and it won't be here forever. How can there be a happy ending when everyone is condemned to death? Things are so *arbitrary*. I identify with the victims, the people who lose. I don't know why I'm not a Bangladeshi. I have an enormous sense of luck. There are a lot of people who could be me, but there's a lot of mystery and luck about it. Ninety-nine per cent of the world's creatures lose. The fact that I won doesn't have to do with anything except luck. I fear that people begrudge that to me. A girl at the CBC found me crying one day. 'You've had so much,' she said, 'you deserve to have some suffering.' I hate that. I've learned to set up barriers, to say 'this far and no further'. I am allowed to commit suicide, but nobody is allowed to kill me."

She is a hunter. She is excited by the chase, by the taste of blood at the kill. She doesn't take cheap shots and she doesn't use booby traps; she plays fair. "I'll take incredible chances," she says, "but I calculate the odds. I won't do something stupid. I'm not suicidal. I won't expose myself to a 70-30 proposition. I know what I can do. You have to be willing to take a chance. How else are you going to develop the muscle? You have to test yourself, you have to have some vested interests. It makes me respect people who have a few things to hide, even from themselves. I never feel guilty about exploiting people. I give something too. You've got to be prepared to take it. I did an interview with Jan Morris, you know, the man who had a sex change. She got at me, she got at me too. 'You're not comfortable with me, are you?' she said. And I had to admit it, 'No, I'm not.' It ended up feeling fair. You can cheat, you can edit that out of the tape, but that's what you have to leave in. That's the bargain. You also have to give yourself."

It's that risk, that whiff of personal danger that Barbara brings to every encounter. "I'm a lot kinder than I was," she says quietly. "I was a child when I started. I know now how adults feel."

About the Authors:

Myrna Kostash, from Edmonton, now leads a hectic life as a University of Toronto teacher, N.F.B. script-writer, and widely-published free-lance writer. She is a regular columnist for *Maclean's*.

Melinda McCracken is a Winnipegger who came east to work on the Toronto *Globe and Mail*, before turning to free-lance writing. Her first book, *Memories Are Made of This*, has just been published.

Valerie Miner has published widely in magazines in Canada (*Saturday Night*), the U.S. (*Saturday Review*), and Britain (*New Society*), and has lived and worked as a writer in all three countries.

Erna Paris, a Toronto native, is a former *Maclean's* staffer who has also worked in radio and TV. Her articles regularly appear in major Canadian magazines such as *Chatelaine*, *Toronto Life*, and *Saturday Night*.

Heather Robertson has worked for the *Winnipeg Tribune* and the C.B.C. and is now a feature-writer and columnist for *Maclean's*. She is the author of three books, *Salt of The Earth*, *Grass Roots*, and *Reservations Are For Indians*.